CHAPTER 1: ELEMENTS OF MARKETING MANAGEMENT

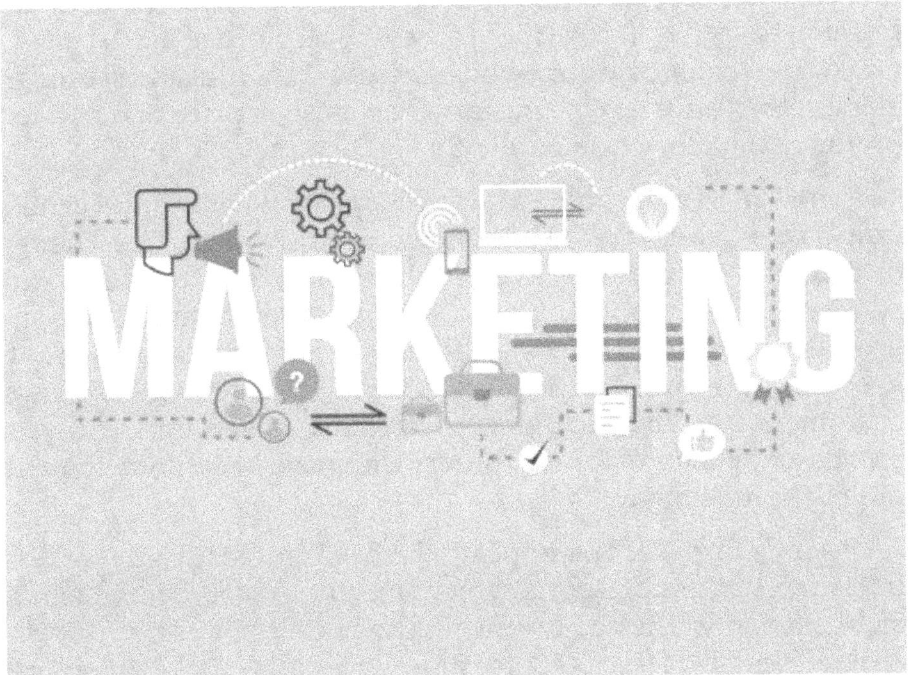

1.1 Introduction
1.2 Meaning of Marketing Management
1.3 Nature & Scope of Marketing Management
1.4 Features of Marketing Management

1.1 Introduction

Every business is in the business of "marketing" itself, its products and services. The subject of marketing therefore makes for interesting study for anyone who wants to succeed in business. If one carefully considers the success of any company, one will find that the company was able to succeed because its marketing efforts ably tied together those of every other department. Marketing revolves around consumers and their needs, its focus enables the business to conceptualize, design, price and deliver products and services accordingly.

The environment in which a business operates has an impact and influence on consumer needs and choices. For instance, the recent COVID-19 crisis has revealed the need for new products and services. This is probably why Swiggy, a food delivery service provider has started offering delivery of groceries and meat. It has also come up with the service "Swiggy Genie" which allows customers to ship parcel and have items picked up. This has proved to be a boon for customers who have been home bound due to the lockdown.

Another example of the impact of the environment on marketing is the success of Zoom, which provides video conferencing facilities and witnessed a surge in the number of users. Google enabled Google Meet, a G-Suite offering for all Gmail users, more people started discovering and using Microsoft Teams, Webex and Telegram. The customer profile of each of these companies evolved to include teachers, students and individuals who were non users of these services earlier. It is not that these services did not exist but that they were not used by as many people as those who are using them right now.

INDEX

*All Images in the book are taken from www.freepik.com

The adverse impact of the pandemic is being felt by many industries and sectors, the hospitality industry and travel and tourism sectors are among some of the worst hit. Fewer people are travelling due to travel restrictions and non availability of transportation. Brands like Airbnb, Marriott, Hilton and Hyatt are feeling the heat of decline in demand. Many hotels are offering future bookings at highly discounted rates; some five star hotel brands have started offering food delivery via Swiggy. This is indicative of a shift in products/services and pricing induced by environmental changes and demand dynamics. This is why every business that succeeds/withstands the test of time and the vagaries of socio-economic, technological and political changes is always one that manages its marketing properly. This is done by seeing every problem as an opportunity to reinvent itself and its products.

Before we explore the concept of Marketing Management, let us consider some definitions of Marketing.

> ***Marketing is the creation and delivery of a standard of living to society. (Paul Mazur)***

Paul Mazur's definition is indicative of the scope of marketing. Through the provision of better products and services, marketing helps to enhance the standard of living enjoyed by society.

For instance wide availability of Smartphones has made it possible for a large section of society to carry out e-commerce transactions, read, learn and of course connect with others through their phones. This has made life convenient for many.

> ***Marketing is not a function. It is the whole business seen from the customer's point of view. (Peter Drucker)***

Peter Drucker's definition presents another perspective on the scope of marketing.

He states that it is not just "one function" but it is the "whole business". This definition amplifies the importance of marketing for businesses. It also highlights the importance of the "customer". Seeing things from the customer's perspective helps a business to spot the gaps that need to be serviced. As mentioned earlier,

Swiggy, a restaurant delivery service was able to see the need for door delivery of groceries, dairy and meats for customers during the lockdown.

Marketing is the performance of all business activities that direct the flow of goods and services from the producer to the consumer. (American Marketing Association)

One of the earlier definitions of Marketing by the AMA (American Marketing Association) presents a comprehensive view of marketing. It states that marketing encompasses all the activities that are performed between production and sales. Essentially it states that marketing is what happens between making a product, selling it and consuming it. With time, this definition of marketing has evolved.

AN INTERESTING FACT

** The AMA's definitions of marketing and marketing research are reviewed and reapproved/modified every three-years by a panel of five scholars who are active researchers.*

** Marketing is the activity, set of institutions, and processes for creating, communicating, delivering, and exchanging offerings that have value for customers, clients, partners, and society at large. (AMA, 2017)*

** "Marketing is an administrative and social process through which individuals and groups obtain what they need and desire by the generation, offering and exchange of valuable products with their equals". Philip Kotler*

** A social and managerial process by which individuals and groups obtain what they need and want through creating and exchanging products and value with each other Kotler, Armstrong, Saunders and Wong, (2001:5)*

After reading this you should be able to-

a. Interpret/explain some frequently cited definitions of Marketing?

b. Develop your own definition of "Marketing".

1.2 Meaning of Marketing Management

Having considered some definitions of marketing and their interpretations, one thing that stands out is that marketing is an all pervasive influence of business. No business can afford to ignore it, if it wants to succeed and continue to exist. Now let us try to decipher the concept of Marketing Management, an amalgamation of "Marketing" and "Management". Management is the art of getting things done through others. It involves mobilizing and maneuvering the 4 M's: men, money, machinery and materials. It encompasses the functions of planning, organizing, staffing, directing, coordinating and controlling.

Thus, Marketing Management involves the following:

1. Defining marketing objectives
2. Devising marketing plans
3. Organizing various aspects of the business to achieve these objectives and implement plans
4. Managing the personnel involved in marketing for the business
5. Directing people, units/departments appropriately
6. Coordinating activities, people and departments
7. Controlling performance to ensure compliance with objectives and plans

Let us consider some significant definitions of Marketing Management:

"Marketing management is the analysis, planning, implementation and control of programmes designed to bring about desired exchanges with target markets for the purpose of achieving organizational objectives. It relies heavily on designing the organizations offering in terms of the target markets needs and desires and using effective pricing, communication, and distribution to inform, motivate and service the market." (Philip Kotler)

"The art and science of choosing target markets and getting, keeping, and growing customers through creating, delivering, and communicating superior customer value" by Kotler and Keller.

1.3 Nature & Scope of Marketing Management

Very simply put Marketing Management is marketing in action. It is a business process that facilitates exchange while delivering value and customer satisfaction. It is the science of understanding customer wants and needs. It is the art of communicating and convincing customers, competing effectively and efficiently, managing people and resources involved in the process.

The Scope of Marketing Management is very wide and includes the following:

1.   **Establishment of Marketing Goals/Objectives:** Objectives are the basis of planning. Like a lighthouse that guides ships to the shore, well defined goals enable a firm to outline its plan of action. These goals/objectives may be long term/short term/ qualitative/quantitative.

2.   **Selection of Target Market:** This involves identifying specific groups of customers and servicing their needs and requirements. Understanding who your customer is, what age, gender, income group, thinking, understand, perceived value and expectations is part of this process. For instance the target market for Mercedes Benz is very different from that of a Maruti Suzuki. The customer profile for Maruti Suzuki Arena and Nexa range of cars is different.

3.   **Determination of Suitable Organisation Structure:** Depending on its products, target market and availability of resources a firm will have to define an organisation structure accordingly. Broad alternatives include product, function, matrix/geographical organisation structures.

4. **Good Internal and External Relations:** The smooth conduct of business operations requires good relations between internal departments/units and external parties such as intermediaries, advertisers, customers and society in general. The goodwill of all concerned is necessary.

5. **Marketing Research:** Adequate, relevant and accurate information is the basis for good marketing planning. Marketing research provides information relating to the target market, competition, intermediaries, pricing and trends to refine marketing plans.

6. **Sales Management:** All business success hinges on a firm's ability to "sell" its products/services. Defining sales targets, training sales force, motivating them and guiding them while executing sales and meeting targets is an important aspect of marketing management.

7. **Control:** The control of marketing operations ensures that objectives are met in the most effective and efficient manner.

1.4 Features of Marketing Management

1. It is an amalgamation of the disciplines of Marketing and Management: It involves planning, organizing, staffing, directing, coordinating and controlling of a firm's marketing operations and processes.

2. It is a Continuous Process: In order to stay relevant, competitive, efficient and productive a firm must continuously revise and refine is objectives, plans and ensure proper implantation.

3. It precedes Production and follows Sales: This is because it starts with defining the target market, identifying its characteristics, needs and wants, developing products and services accordingly, pricing, promoting and distributing them in sync with the market and resources available. It does not end with sales but extends to customer satisfaction, delight and after sales behavior.

4. It revolves around the customer: Every aspect of marketing management focuses on the customer. It starts with studying and profiling customers and ends with delivering value and ensuring customer delight.

5. It is an Art and Science: It involves the application of economic, financial, socio-economic and psychological theories to marketing efforts. It is primarily concerned with people and what drives/motivates them. The definition by Kotler and Keller cited earlier sheds light on this aspect of Marketing Management.

1.5 Functions of Marketing Management

1. Marketing Research: Is a focused endeavor that a company undertakes to collect information regarding its target market. This helps the company to understand customer needs and requirements, test the response to its products/services, make better pricing, promotion and distribution decisions. It enables a firm to discover gaps in the market and service them. It helps a company to improve its products and services as well as overall marketing efforts.

2. Customer Profiling: A customer profile/buyer persona is complete, factual information about customers with regard to demography, buyer behavior, customer service interactions, expectations and satisfaction. Customer profiling is the process of creating a buyer persona.

3. Product Planning and Development: The product/service is the core of the offering that a company makes to its target market. For instance creating a range of cold pressed oils and millet based foods for a customer base comprising health conscious people who would not mind paying more for a health food item. Similarly a fitness/yoga app is something that would appeal to health conscious people. Creating a product/service that is in line with customer needs/wants/expectations is the essence of good product planning and development.

4. Sourcing/Buying and Assembly: The manufacturing process requires inputs, supplies, components, spare parts, packaging material. These will have to be sourced in appropriate quantity and quality and assembled or processed to create finished products and services.

5. Storage: Suitable storage facility for raw material, components, spare parts, accessories, packaging material and finished goods is necessary to maintain quality and steady supply to and from the firm.

6. Transportation/Logistics: The movement of workforce, raw material, components, spare parts, accessories, packaging material and finished goods is necessary to maintain a steady flow of the same to and from the firm.

7. Pricing: Pricing is a critical decision for any firm. The right price will attract customers to products/services. The decision to be a market leader/follower as far as price goes is one which every firm must take.

8. Sales Forecasting: This function enables a firm to estimate its future sales. Accuracy in sales forecasting equips a firm in turn to make accurate business decisions and predict long term and short term performance. Past sales related data, industry information and economic trends provide the basis for carrying out sales forecasting.

9. Advertising: Advertising is an important function that builds brand awareness, informs and educates customers about availability of products/services/offers/pricing. It helps businesses and organisations to influence the behavior and thereby the quality of life enjoyed by customers in particular and society in general. It does not just sell products and services; it sells ideas about better thoughts and actions for society as whole.

10. Sales Promotion: It comprises short-term tactics/initiatives employed by a company to boost sales. Discounts, coupons, contests, exchange offers are some instances of sales promotion initiatives taken by companies to introduce new products, revive sales, attract more customers and undertake stock clearance.

11. Personal Selling/Salesmanship: This refers to face-to-face interaction between salespersons and customers. Salesmanship is the oldest form of traditional sales. Sales personnel assist customers in making informed purchase decisions. The purchase of electronic items, automobiles and pharmaceutical products are some cases in which the advice and information provided by the salesman helps customers to make a good purchase decision.

12. Distribution: This activity helps products to reach customers/final users/beneficiaries. Logistics helps to remove bottlenecks in the distribution process. With the surge in E-commerce transactions the importance of this activity has only increased. Hindustan Unilever Limited is a pioneer in mobile van sales of its products in the Indian rural market. It was able to penetrate rural markets because it worked on improving its distribution.

13.   Packaging and Labeling: Packages help to keep products safe and fresh through transportation and until they are used. Some packages facilitate storage of products until they are consumed. Packages also facilitate product differentiation and identification making it easier for buyers to locate products in a store/ on store shelves. Labels provide information regarding ingredients, instructions for use, price, name and address of manufacturer, date of manufacture and expiry date. Packaging is the sum total of all the activities that contribute to designing and producing the package for a product. In recent times the scope of packaging has extended to attention to disposal and recycling.

14.   Social Media Marketing: With the wide penetration of the internet, cheaper data packs, widespread availability of Wi-fi facilities and increasing number of social media users, social media marketing has become imperative for any brand wanting to consolidate its presence in the market. The use of social networks like Facebook, Instagram, YouTube, Pinterest, WhatsApp, Twitter, etc to promote products and services has increased. The tribe of "influencers" is found in the social media space and used to exert influence on social media users who could be "followers" of such influencers.

15.   Digital Marketing: Digital marketing includes social media marketing. Its scope includes digital devices like television, Smartphones, tablets, gaming devices, desktop computers, social media platforms like the ones mentioned in the previous point, websites, e-mail marketing, blogs and so on. Digital marketing means marketing on digital media, platforms and/technology.

16.   After Sales Service: A lot of consumer satisfaction/dissatisfaction depends on after sales service and grievance redressal by a company. After sales service to maintain products like automobiles and electronics is a big part of the post purchase experience for any customer. Grievance redressal for faulty/defective products must be given due attention to avoid customer dissatisfaction.

<u>**A CASE IN POINT**</u>

** PETA marketing campaigns always include a documentation of the conditions showing how animals are treated in various conditions, with the intention of shedding light to what would otherwise be considered as normal social practices or lifestyles where people don't realize that animals are being brutally killed in order to bring them things we use on a daily basis.*
Looking back, PETA has come up with a number of creative marketing strategies over the years

1.6 Components of Marketing Management

Marketing and its management is almost as diverse a field as business management itself. The main components of marketing consist of analysis, planning, implementation and control (Czinkota & Ronkainen, 2007). These are the components no matter what the kind of industry or service the target of marketing might be.

Situational/Strategic Analysis

A strategic analysis is always carried out in a certain context. It is a snapshot of where a company is and where it stands in the market. A good anlaysis should be comprehensive and include internal and external factors. It should be powered by reliable quantitative and qualitative data and information from primary and secondary sources.

Strategy Planning

A marketing strategy is a tactical and competitive plan which is the outcome of situational analysis. It defines goals and objectives, ways and means to achieve them and the resources and efforts that will be required to reach those goals. A strategy might require internal adjustments, structural changes, the procurement of greater/better resources, modifications in product/service, distribution, pricing and promotion. A good strategy is not only about having a definite plan A but also about coming up with alternative plans that can be employed in case plan A fails/encounters roadblocks.

Strategy Implementation and Control

No strategy or plan is effective if it remains on paper; implementation is important. Implementation impacts every member and department of the company, it demands their involvement and depends on their contribution/participation. Effective implementation calls for frequent evaluation and re-evaluation of plans if necessary. A strategy may pertain to product innovation, cost leadership, promotion and/or distribution or to changes within the organisation like its functioning and managerial aspects. All other aspects of managing a business depend on the effectiveness of its marketing strategy.

1.7 Problems of Marketing Management

1. **Dynamic Environment:** One of the biggest challenges for any firm and its marketing efforts is the fact that it exists within a dynamic environment. Political unrest within a country/state or political discord between nations can pose challenges and present opportunities. The recent Indo-China tensions are an opportunity for Indian buyers to go the *swadeshi* route and opt for Indian products. Instead of getting a Chinese Smartphone one can consider the purchase of any other brand/make

from India or any country other than China.

The COVID-19 crisis is an opportunity to develop better health care services and sanitation products. Food and home delivery apps and e-commerce companies became frontline heroes in a market space where local *kirana* stores, mom and pop shops and malls dominated the supply of groceries and consumables. Cinema halls ran out of business opportunities but the demand for subscription based online streaming services like Netflix, Amazon Prime and Disney Hot star among others grew.

The demand for automobiles plummeted and big players like Hero Motocorp, Bajaj Auto, Suzuki, and TVS Motors reported a drastic fall in their year-on-year sales figures for March 2020. The point here is that no can really prepare themselves to meet the dynamism of the business environment.

2. **Staying on Top of Trends:** Trends are important for businesses because they keep changing. Their impact can have far reaching consequences. A growing work from home culture will result in decreased demand for real estate space for companies. An e-commerce boom means one can do business without a physical store but only with the support of a good logistics and supply chain. It also means that the launch of the iPhone Pro 11 in September 2019 set an important trend- that of 3 cameras in one phone. For a long time now the camera quality of a phone has been an important criterion for Smartphone buyers. Never before did one phone offer 3 cameras but thereafter this became a trend. Particularly in the field of technology, one finds that new phones are launched multiple times a year because people change handsets very frequently and are looking for new features.

The fashion industry is another arena in which new designs are launched very season-spring, summer and winter collections set new trends and call for fresh wardrobes for those who follow those trends. Staying on top of trends and predicting them with accuracy are difficult tasks for any business.

3. **Demand Generation:** Getting people to buy is the challenge every business faces. For staples this might not be a problem but in case of products that require research and investment demand generation is a problem. Convincing people to buy bread and milk might not be a challenge but getting people to buy real estate and automobiles is a bigger challenge.

Another important factor is that demand is situational. For instance a face mask was not an item purchased by everyone but today after the COVID-19 crisis has struck it has become a necessity, even a fashion statement as wedding clothes designers are making masks to match wedding outfits. Surgical masks are being purchased by common people because they are easier to tolerate when compared to cotton/cloth masks. The demand for soaps, sanitizers and disinfectants has grown; everyone needs one and is using more than usual. In an economic downturn such as this demand generation is a bigger problem, with loss of income/salary cuts being a widespread phenomenon people's ability to spend has shrunk.

4. **Competition and Market Share:** All businesses must contend with competition and try to retain if not expand their market share. This is important if they want to maintain/increase sales. The Surf-Tide and Coke-Pepsi brand wars are the perfect example of competition and a fight for market share. Some brands like magi noodles did not have to worry about market share because they enjoyed a near monopoly. Brands like Netflix have chosen to be sensitive to subscribers and instead of cashing in on the opportunity that the pandemic has offered-more people staying indoors and the possibility of increase in the demand for its services, the brand has chosen to discontinue subscriptions of inactive users.

This move aims at reducing unnecessary expenditure

5. **Finding Customers and Retaining Them:** Timeless brands like Lux, Dove and Pears soap have done a great job on this front. Not only have they found customers but they have kept people engaged with their commitment to beauty with a purpose while taking care to establish an emotional connect with audiences. Customer retention is achieved by refreshing product lines so from a soap product lines have expanded to liquid soaps, shampoos, creams, conditioners, lotions, etc.

Finding customers perhaps is less challenging when compared to retaining them primarily because the number of alternatives a customer has a numerous. Customer retention through loyalty programs and membership cards are widely used by malls, departmental stores, coupons and price offs are used in e-commerce. Pre-approved loans offered by banks to existing customers, loans at attractive rates, free debit cards are all examples of customer retention strategies used by banks.

6. **Public Relations:** The importance of public relations really stands out during a business crisis. Companies like Nestle and Cadbury were able to tide over their crises only because of their initiatives to maintain good public relations. This was an important aspect of the comeback staged by Maggi noodles and Cadbury Dairy Milk. It is not only companies but even political parties that gain from good public realtions. The *chai pe charcha* endeavour is a public relations campaign that uses Narendra Modi, the most powerful influencer in the BJP (*Bharatiya Janta* Party) to have a conversation with the general public.

7. **Developing the Right Narrative:** The narrative of a brand or company is the story that it wants to tell the customers about its products/services/what it stands for. It is a conversation that the company has with its target market in particular and the world at large. The

Nike advertising campaign is a good example of a timeless narrative. The brand has been urging people to get up and "Just Do It" since 1987. Just Do it is more than a tagline it is a fitness *mantra* that Nike wants people to adopt, make fitness your lifestyle is what their advertisements say. Similarly the "Got Milk" campaign which was launched in 1993 is another really good example of a great narrative. Celebrities and cartoon characters with a milk moustache sold the idea and benefits of drinking milk every day have been featuring in this American advertising campaign to encourage the consumption of milk.

8. **Defining your USP (Unique Selling Proposition):** In an intensely competitive market your USP is what makes or breaks the deal. People want to know what it is that you offer, why they should buy "your" product/service when they have so many other alternatives. You will find that people prefer the domestic flyer Indigo airlines, over other airlines because it is always on time. Punctuality of the airline is what sets it apart because being on time matters when you have business meetings or important events to catch. The USP of a restaurant could be delicious food at affordable prices supplemented by cleanliness, courteous staff, ambience. Your USP is what distinguishes you. Defining it carefully is important. For instance Dove soap advertisements always say Dove is one quarter moisturizing cream; its USP is the goodness of moisturizing cream.

9. **Refreshing Products/Product lines:** If you want to retain the "interest" of customers then you have to keep refreshing your product/product lines. If you want to compete then you have to add newer and better products. You might also have to tweak your pricing. If you are selling butter then you might want to add white butter, herb butter and even nut butters like almond and peanut to your brand arsenal. While you might still

have loyal customers if you do not add new products you might not be able to attract new customers with different food choices with the same old product.

10.   Staying Relevant: Keeping up with the times and stay relevant to evolving lifestyles and technological advancements is necessary to survive in business. Detergent brands today are a good example of this. From bars of soap to liquid detergents, detergent powders in various fragrances and to suit every washing machine be it front load or top load, they have evolved to stay relevant. As long as people hand washed clothes it was okay to have detergent is soap or powder form but with the growing number of washing machines in household promoted the addition of a whole host of variations with enzyme technology and the benefits of gentle on fabrics and powerful stain removal.

1.8 Marketing Management Philosophy

Traditional

Production Concept: According to this concept accompany will undertake mass production of goods and take advantage of the economies of scale that accrue thereof. Mass production will lower cost of production making it possible to sell the goods at lower prices and earn profits.

The limitation of this concept is that-low prices might not be the only consideration for a customer. For instance people will not look for low cost when opting for health care. Here quality will be an important consideration. If a customer is buying a wedding gown she will look for differentiation, it will have emotional significance for her, price might not be an important consideration.

Product Concept

The product concept differs from the production concept because it considers quality and innovation as major factors influencing customers rather than price and availability of a product/

service. This is why designer products and labels are preferred by people over and above standardized products. A custom made car by someone like Dilip Chabbria will be coveted by someone who wants the exclusivity that a one of a kind product offers. The cost of such a car or designer item may be much more but its quality/innovation could be the reason why a customer will prefer to have it.

Selling Concept

In the selling concept "sales" are the focus. A customer is to be persuaded by buy the product (sales are induced) by all means necessary. Companies aligned with the selling concept have a short-term objective of making a sale rather than a long-term objective of building brand loyalty, creating customer satisfaction and customer retention. Aggressive selling, intensive advertising, sales promotion and publicity is undertaken. If required, customers are manipulated to buy products/services. For example image manipulation in advertisements for weight loss, false claims about oils that promote hair growth and beauty products that can lighten skin tones.

Contemporary

Marketing Concept

The marketing concept revolves around the customer. Everything begins and ends with the customer. Defining the target market and buyer persona, determining needs and wants, pricing, influencing, convincing, selling and ensuring customer satisfaction and delight, whatever a firm does is done keeping the customer in mind. For instance the "no questions asked returns policy" followed by most E-commerce players could be a manifestation of the marketing concept in business.

Societal Marketing Process

The societal marketing concept propounds the creation of products that will satisfy customer needs without harming the environment. For instance doing away with plastic bags and using jute/cloth bags, replacing plastic toothbrushes with bamboo toothbrushes, using solar lamps and solar energy. Such choices empower the customer to fulfill his/her needs while reducing his/her carbon footprint.

1.9 Marketing Characteristics in Indian Context

1. Dynamic environment: The Indian business environment as a whole is an extremely dynamic one. As a nation India presents immense possibilities and innumerable challenges to marketers. Fluid socio-economic, political and technological changes keep marketers engaged in coming up with ways and means to influence consumers. Today it is possible for businesses to retail across India without a physical store. At the other end of the spectrum, customers can buy almost any product at the click of a button. Between these two entities, the manufacturer and the consumer lie facilitators and agencies like websites, e-commerce platforms, various advertising media, tools and technologies, distribution networks and logistics. From selling products and services to concepts, ideologies and entertainment the realm of marketing in India has expanded and evolved in ways no one thought possible even a few years ago.

2. The Growth of Organised Retail: Malls and departmental stores that dot cityscapes across the country have changed the way India shops. These organized retail spaces stock and sell some of the best Indian and global brands. They are the hub not only for shopping but for entertainment and food. The growth of organized retail has offered local small shops and stores the opportunity to evolve and improve their marketing efforts. Their customer relationship management, friendly approach, credit policies and home delivery makes them the go to sources to procure essentials and items of daily use for many customers.

3. Informed Consumers: Consumers today are more informed and aware. The mobile phone and internet penetration has put huge amounts of information within the reach of buyers even in small towns and villages. Customer reviews and feedback have a critical role to play now particularly in e-commerce transactions where bad reviews can derail sales. In fact people look for reviews and make decisions based on the same.

4. Increasing E-commerce Transactions: It is now possible to buy everything from a pin to an automobile to cars and diamonds online. Where you live does not restrict your access to products and services. There is an app for every need and right from reading your daily news to keeping track of your diet and fitness, everything is possible from the palm of your hand-through your mobile phone.

5. Shift in the Power Centers of Decision Making: Women and children are exerting greater influence in purchase decisions. With greater financial independence women are able to decide about more than buying groceries and detergents for their homes. An informed next generation is actively involved in purchase decisions for all sorts of products and services consumed by a family.

6. Demographic Shift: An increase in the number of young, working people and women has made these market segments attractive target markets for a number of companies. A large number of senior citizens and nuclear family structures has spurred the growth of products and services across housing, health care, electronics, food, banking, insurance, etc.

7. Service Sector Growth: This has enhanced the need to focus on customer satisfaction and delight. Segments like the wedding planning and services business is an example. The professionalization of every little aspect from food, décor, make up, photography to gifting has created immense possibilities. Services like handymen to repair things and run errands are available and suddenly services are no longer just banking, insurance, finance and education, they are much more.

8. Surge in Social Media Marketing and Digital Marketing Initiatives: Byproducts of technological advancement and internet penetration, social media marketing and digital marketing have become a necessity for every company and brand that wants to stay relevant and enhance visibility. Presence across digital platforms and social media networks is a must, not an option even if you want to market a film or a sporting event.

9. Beyond Products and Services: Marketing in India has evolved beyond products and services to marketing ideas and ideologies. Whether it is the campaign to promote consumption of eggs, vegan lifestyle, prevention of cruelty to animals or campaigns by political parties which popularized ideas like " *ab ki baar Modi sarkar"*, *"aam aadmi"* to brands like Amul which has chosen to keep its finger on the pulse of India, marketing has been enriched with much more than the sole objective of "selling". Sporting events like the IPL (Indian Premiere League) and cultural events like the *Kumbh Mela* have become sought after platforms for brands looking to make a mark creatively and cash in on footfall and viewership at such events.

10. The humanization of brands: Informed and enlightened marketers have realized the significance of humanizing brands. Tata Steel has always put the spotlight on its people, the employees who make the company what it is. Their tagline "We also make steel" amplifies their commitment to and focus on "people" rather than their "product". Brands like Amul have a unique voice. Their campaign does not sell 'butter" it talks about the joys, sorrows, achievements, failures of India in particular and the world at large.

11. The power of the internet: extends "equal opportunity" all Indians to avail of products and services transcending geographical, socio-economic and political boundaries/barriers.

12. Rural Markets and Towns as Retail Destinations: The saturation of the urban market and intense competition have compelled marketers to look at rural markets and Tier II and Tier III cities as the next big retail destinations. While Hindustan Unilever and ITC have made inroads into the rural hinterlands quite some time back, e-commerce players like Amazon, Flipkart, Nykaa and Firstcry are catering to people from villages and small towns.

1.10 Marketing Management Process

As mentioned in the introduction, marketing is contextual. It depends on the customer and environment. The marketing management process comprises 4 steps:

1. Situational Analysis: Every company has its own unique situation encompassing internal and external factors. It has an internal environment and it is always responding to/adapting to/ impacted by the external environment. PEST (Political, Economic, Social and Technological factors) analysis or PESTEL in marketing provides a model for situation analysis. **PEST Analysis** is a measurement tool which is used to assess markets for a particular product or a business within/with reference to a given time frame. Similarly a SWOT (Strengths weaknesses, opportunities and threats) analysis helps a company to take stock of its internal resources, products and offerings as well as external conditions. A situational analysis can be a wakeup call to make some significant changes in the way business is carried on.

2. Marketing Strategy: A **marketing strategy** refers to a business's overall game plan to gain competitive advantage. A good strategy makes it possible for a business to reach prospective consumers and turn them into users of its products/services, For best results a strategy can be multi-pronged ie. It can be a combination of product, price, distribution and promotional strategies.

3. Marketing Mix Decisions: The **marketing mix** of a company is a set of controllable variables and their levels which a firm uses to influence its target market. The marketing mix helps a business to continuously evaluate and re-evaluate itself. Traditionally the marketing mix had just 4 elements- product, price, promotion, place, these 4 P's have now become a 7 P formulas with the addition of packaging, positioning and people to it.

4. Implementation and Control: Once the strategy has been devised a marketing plan/set of plans is in place implementation follows. Having a good plan is not enough; it must be put into action. While implanting plans care should be taken to ensure that deviations are corrected and things are on track. Sudden changes and unexpected developments like the COVID-19 crisis have hit small and big businesses and could not have really been taken into account when planning, these can be viewed as opportunities to renew and refresh a business and its offerings. Such times call for revision of the marketing mix.

CASE STUDY: TANISHQ

In the mid-1990s the Tata group conducted a survey, which revealed that jewellery was gaining popularity as an essential fashion statement. While there were number of small and medium jewellers catering to the market, they discovered that unethical practices like under-karating had sullied the segment. Titan decided to enter the market with the assurance of a brand.

Customer education and changes in perception were used by the Tata group to make inroads in to a market dominated by traditional or family jewellers. Established in 1994, Tanishq has followed a two-pronged brand-building strategy of cultivating trust by educating customers on the unethical practices encountered in the business and the use of innovative methods to change the perception of jewellery as a high-priced product. This empowered the company to alter its customer base to include the working urban woman and helped the brand to service the needs of buyers for jewellery during festivals as well as work and other casual occasions.

Over time, Tanishq has added to its range of products on offer with the likes of Zoya and GoldPlus added to its collection. Its range of products includes casual wear, fine jewellery in diamond, platinum and gold.

Consumers today realize the importance of diamond certification and BIS hallmarked jewellery as a quality initiative offered by all branded players.

The introduction of lower priced jewellery enabled Tanishq to cater to the affordable jewellery segment. They launched the Mia brand of gold and diamond jewellery for working women priced at Rs 6,000-50,000. Subsequently, it launched the FQ brand of diamonds with a starting price of INR 499 aimed at teenagers.

Installment schemes have also been introduced to facilitate purchase of jewellery.

Multiple distribution methods are being used. Earlier Tanishq operated through exclusive company opened showrooms but now has adopted the franchisee business model and has a structured programme covering induction, product and business related training for franchisees and their staff.

Tanishq retails through its website. It digital campaigns and in-film placement have consolidated brand recall. Since 2016 Caratlane, has become a subsidiary of Tanishq and this has boosted its online reach.

Tanishq uses print, outdoor and television to advertise its products. It has also created an exclusive range of jewellery for Bollywood films Jodhaa Akbar and Paheli.

Value Added Services have made an impact. The introduction of value added services such as certification of gold and diamonds, lifetime return and buy-back scheme has further fuelled the growth of the organised jewellery segment. Such trade practices have resulted in the perception of superior quality associated with branded jewellery.

All major brands actively use social media platforms like Facebook and Twitter for promotional activities and have websites and online stores. Allied promotional endeavours like the mobile makeover van Tanishq used to launch its Mia brand of low cost jewellery are also being used.

CHAPTER 2: MARKETING STRATEGY AND CONSUMER BEHAVIOUR

2.1 Marketing Strategy
2.1.1 Introduction
2.1.2 Concept of Strategy
2.1.3 Meaning of Marketing Strategy

2.1.4 Significance of Marketing Strategy
2.1.5 Aim of Marketing Strategy
2.1.6 Marketing Strategy Formulation
2.1.7 Bases of Formulating Marketing Strategy
2.1.8 Types of Marketing Strategy

2.1.1 Introduction

The marketing environment comprises a number of controllable and uncontrollable factors. Competition is something all businesses barring monopolies must contend with. A well established chain of hotels would have not foreseen the competition it faces from an Airbnb. Similarly an Idea or Vodafone might not have seen Reliance as formidable competition till a Jio came along. Competition necessitates marketing strategies which are plans to counter competition.

2.1.2 Concept of Strategy

Strategy has its origins in the context of military action/warfare/combat/battle. The word "strategy" is derived from the Greek word "stratçgos"; stratus (meaning army) and "ago" (meaning leading/moving).**In the context of business, a Strategy** refers to an action/set of actions that managers take to attain one or more organizational goals. It also refers to competitive plans of a business.

Strategy can be defined as "A general direction set for the company and its various components to achieve a desired state in the future. Strategy results from the detailed strategic planning process."

A strategy is the blueprint of organisational decisions that indicates its goals and objectives, outlines key policies and plans for the achievement of goals. It defines the type of business to be carried out, the overall objective of what type of organisation a company wants to be seen as whether and how it wants to contribute to stakeholders and society.

A strategy involves the integration of organizational activities to utilize and allocate scarce resources within the organizational environment so as to meet the present objectives. Strategies are not formulated in a vacuum simply because a firm does not function is isolation. A firm's actions firm impact and draw reactions from those affected such actions. The affected parties include employees, suppliers, competitors and customers.

A strategy is always goal directed and in business that goal may be to stay ahead of the competition or to retain market share. The attainment of these goals however is subject to uncertainty of circumstances and behavior of consumers and competitors.

Features of Strategy

1. **A Strategy is Forward Looking:** While it is not possible to accurately predict the future, a strategy is significant because it is predictive in its approach and has to consider critical and largely uncontrollable factors.

2. **A Strategy is concerned with long term and critical developments:** Its importance stems from the fact that a strategy is concerned with non-routine aspects of business like innovations in production/products/pricing/packaging/venturing into new markets.

3. **A Strategy is concerned with Unpredictable factors:** A large part of strategic initiatives hinge on unpredictability of the behavior of customers/competitors/employees.

4. **A strategy is a road map:** It guides an organisation along the direction of its goals and objectives. It nudges an organization along the path of progress.

5. **A strategy is a bridge:** between where an organisation is

and where it wants to go.

2.1.3 Meaning of Marketing Strategy

A marketing strategy is a competitive plan that enables a firm to operate with long-term profitability. It guides a firm towards the attainment of its marketing objectives while ensuring optimum utilization of resources and enhancing the sale of products/services. It is the foundation of a company's marketing plan.

It comprises:

1. A company's value proposition
2. Key brand promise and message
3. Data on consumer profiles
4. Resource capabilities
5. The most profitable route to profits

"Marketing Strategy is defined as an organization's strategy that combines all of its marketing goals into one comprehensive plan".

Marketing Strategy is the Marketing Logic by which the business unit expects to achieve its Marketing Objectives. (Phillip Kotler)

Michael E. Porter, "Marketing strategy has mainly one aim to cope with competition .... There are five major and vital forces that decide the nature and intensity of competition the threat of new entrants, bargaining power of customers, and bargaining power of suppliers, threat of substitute products and the jockeying among the existing contestants.... The collective strength of these forces determines the ultimate profit potential of an industry. And the strategist's goal is to find a position in the industry where his company can best defend itself against these forces or can influence them in his company's favour.... Strategy can be viewed as building defence against the competitive forces."

2.1.4 Significance of Marketing Strategy

1. Helps a firm gain a competitive edge:

A marketing strategy equips a firm to gain a competitive edge in the market. It arms businesses to compete with new entrants and existing competition. This is achieved by outlining the USP (Unique Selling Proposition) in terms of product/service features and benefits in the context of competitors. This enables a firm to establish its unique identity in a dynamic and intensely competitive market. Paper Boat, India's very own traditional drinks company ensured that its USP was strong-traditional drinks that stirred up nostalgia.

2. Generate Awareness

Unique and interesting products facilitate high brand recall. For this the strategic approach helps by highlighting a product/service's USP, features, the legacy or vision of a company. For example Tata Steel portrays its USP as "people" first and then states that "We also make steel", the Venky's ready to eat range of products sold the idea of "Venky's chicken in minutes" to a society where time has become the rarest commodity.

3. Building a New Customer Base Every Time

With regard to customers every company has 2 significant goals-customer retention and attracting new customers. Towards this end the company must study customer's needs, requirements, expectations and aspirations. Regular customer profiling (demographic, socio-economic and psychographic) must be undertaken with the objective of redefining target markets and expanding the customer base.

4. Preparation of marketing budgets

The formulation of a marketing strategy helps to plan the utilization of finance, an important resource for a business. This is achieved through better budgeting, judicious investments and eliminating activities with low/no returns.

5. Unifies the efforts of all departments

A marketing strategy unifies the working of all departments to ensure that they are aligned with it. It integrates traditional and contemporary marketing efforts and ensures that all activities/ functions and tasks are performed in unison.

To put it briefly, a marketing strategy is significant because it:

- Gives the organization a competitive edge.
- Facilitates the development of profitable products and services
- Ensures that organisational planning is carried out with the objective of satisfying customer needs.
- Identifies the internal and external impact of a brand's growth.
- Fixes right price.
- Facilitates optimum utilization of resources.
- Aids efficient budgeting practices.
- Outlines the scope of the marketing plan.
- Facilitates departmental coordination.
- Helps an organisation meet its predetermined objectives.

2.1.5 Aim of Marketing Strategy
The aim of a marketing strategy can be expressed in the form of its objectives:

- To Increase sales and profits
- Building brand awareness

- Increasing market share
- Customer Retention
- Launching new products/services
- Targeting new customers
- Entering new markets locally/globally
- Improving stakeholder relations
- Improving customer relationships
- Improving internal communications and coordination

Needless to say all Marketing Objectives must be SMART:

- Specific
- Measureable
- Achievable
- Realistic
- Time-bound

This is significant because measurable objectives can be monitored and guide the development of plans to meet the business goals.

2.1.6 Marketing Strategy Formulation

The formulation of a Marketing Strategy is an activity that requires the investment of time and effort. Since a strategy forms the basis of an effective plan due attention must be paid to formulating it. The following steps lead up to creation of a marketing strategy:

1. SWOT Analysis: This helps to identify a firm's strengths, weaknesses, opportunities and threats.
2. Determine the Value proposition: This comprises the main strengths of a business and can be determined on the basis of a SWOT analysis.
3. Definition of objectives: SMART objectives to be precise specific, measurable, achievable, realistic

and time bound.

4. Understanding your customers/target audience
5. Creating buyer personas: they are fictional, generalized representations of a firm's ideal customers that humanize the target audience and help marketers to understand them better.
6. Market and Competitor Analysis
7. Establishment of marketing methods

2.1.7 Bases of Formulating Marketing Strategy

A Marketing Strategy formulated on the following bases:

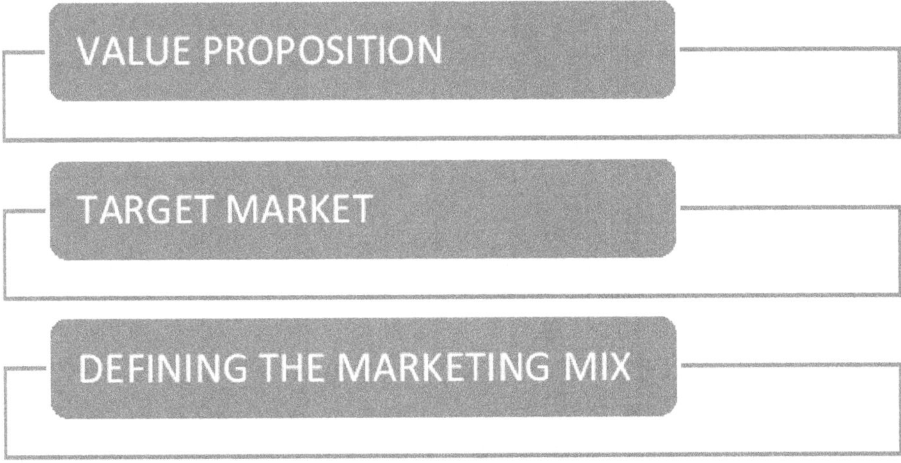

1. A Company's Value Proposition: This is the competitive advantage a company enjoys. For instance Amul's Value Proposition is "Value for Many" being a cooperative movement its aim has been to create value for dairy farmers and deliver quality to customers at very affordable prices. Similarly D Mart offers **Daily Discounts Daily Savings and its functioning revolves around that idea.**

2. Target Market: In depth marketing research helps a firm to gain insights into consumers. It facilitates the segmentation and profiling efforts of a company to identify the most profitable segment for the company and helps refine its promotion and distribution efforts. For instance **the *Shakti* initiative by *Hindustan Unilever* Limited (*HUL*) pioneered the concept of training local women as *rural* sales agents who sell Unilever products door to door in their communities.**

3. Defining the marketing mix: The marketing mix is a set of controllable variables and their levels which a firm uses to influence its target market. Usually the product/service is the most important element of the marketing mix and decisions relating to price, promotion, and distribution are taken accordingly. However if a firm wants to offer low priced products then its price will dictate how the product is made, distributed and promoted.

2.1.8 Types of Marketing Strategy

Marketing Strategies can be classified/ studied on different bases. From the marketing Mix Perspective there are 4 types of strategies

1. **Product Related Marketing Strategy:** Where the focus is on the product/products. Apple has always been product focused and its marketing hinges on product excellence. The product is planned and produced keeping in mind futuristic needs and expectations of customers while staying ahead many years ahead of the competition. It is always about delivering customer delight through the product and its revolutionary features.

2. **Price related strategy:** This takes into account the target market and its ability to pay. For instance when Tat was planning the production of the Nano their aim was to make a car that cost less than one lakh rupees. This was a really low price limit for a car and followed

the penetration pricing strategy. Opposite to this perhaps is the Mercedes Benz range of automobiles which runs into lakhs of rupees and is targeted at people who can afford to buy a luxury car. Pricing can help a company capture a large market segment or a very small but highly profitable segment.

3. **Promotional strategy** is used to inform, persuade, or remind target audiences about products/services. Title sponsorship of the IPL (Indian Premiere League) is a promotional strategy that mentions the brand every time the tournament is spoken about before, during and after the event. This move is directed towards high recall. Also choices like advertising on television during prime time or in the busiest places like Times Square New York all classify as promotional strategies. .

4. A **distribution strategy** is a method of disseminating goods or services to end-users. The most efficient **distribution** method for your business is the key to increasing revenue, increasing market share and retaining customer loyalty. For instance having an app to deliver online classes is a method whereby an educational service provider can reach a large number of learners.

Porter's Generic Strategies:
Three winning strategies suggested by Michael Porter are:
(a) Overall Cost Leadership:
Here the company works hard to achieve the lowest cost of production and distribution so that it can price lower than its competitors and win a large market share.
(b) Differentiation:
Here the company concentrates on creating a highly differentiated product line and marketing programme so that it comes across as the class leader in the industry. Most customers would prefer to own its brand if its price is not too high.

(c) Focus:

Here the company focuses its effort on servicing a few market segments well rather than going after the whole market.

(d) Operational Excellence:

The company provides superior value by leading its industry in price and convenience. It works to reduce costs and to create a lean and efficient value delivery system. It serves customers who want reliable, good quality products or services but who want them easily and at low cost.

(e) Customer Intimacy:

The company provides superior value by precisely segmenting its market and then tailoring its products or services to match exactly with the needs of targeted customers.

It specializes in satisfying unique customer needs through a close relationship with and intimate knowledge of the customer.

It builds detailed customer databases for segmenting and targeting and empowers those who are willing to respond quickly to customer needs. It serves customers who are willing to pay a premium to get precisely what they want and it will do almost anything to build longer customer loyalty and to capture lifetime value.

(f) Product Leadership:

The company provides superior value by offering a continual stream of leading edge products or services that make their own and competing product obsolete.

It is open to new ideas and relentlessly pursues new solutions and works to reduce cycle times so that it can get new products to market quickly. It serves customers who want state-of-the-art products and services, regardless of the costs in terms of price or convenience.

(ii) Competitive Position in the Target Market:

(a) Market Leader:

The firm in an industry with the largest market share is the market leader. It usually leads other firms in price changes, new product introductions, distribution, coverage and promotion spending.

For example: Coca-Cola Co. has 48.6% of the global carbonated beverages **market**, while PepsiCo Inc. has 20.5%. Therefore, Coca-Cola is the **market leader**, while PepsiCo is a **market leader.**

Apple and Amazon are market leaders.

(b) Market Challenger:

A runner up firm in an industry that is fighting hard to increase its market share.

Pepsi is a good **example** of a **challenger** brand. It ran a series of taste-test campaigns wherein people rated its cola taste higher than Coke's.

Flipkart, India's very own homegrown e-Commerce brand, is an example of a challenger to Amazon.

(c) Market Follower:

A runner up firm in an industry that wants to hold its share without rocking the boat.

Chinese brands that followed the leaders in the mobile phone market are an example of Market followers.

(d) Market Niche:

A firm in an industry that serves small segments that other firms over looks or ignore.

For instance: RAW Pressary a company that makes cold pressed, fresh fruit and vegetable juices serves a market niche in a drinks market dominated by carbonated drinks.

CASE STUDY: UNILEVER AND ITS RURAL MARKETING STRATEGY

HUL (Hindustan Unilever Limited) and its rural marketing initiatives are a great lesson in marketing strategies. HUL entered the Indian markets in 1960. It was among the pioneers of rural marketing in India. Having realized that urban markets are saturated and the rural hinterland offers a huge opportunity, they decided to make inroads into uncharted territory. Their mobile marketing vans are a case in point for clever distribution. The weekly *haat* or markets across villages became an opportunity and reduced the need for as established retail store presence in villages.

Realising that rural consumers want value for money, the company came up with 2 in 1 products like Breeze (shampoo + soap), smaller sizes of reputed brands like the Lux soap 25 grams pack, word of mouth publicity through opinion leaders (village leaders/*gram panchayat* members), and influencers in the rural populace, wall painting, distribution of pamphlets, puppet shows and street plays.

"Khushiyon ki Doli" was a rural marketing initiative that was launched by HUL in three states – Uttar Pradesh, Andhra Pradesh and Maharashtra in March 2010.

The main objective of this initiative was to reach out to villages that have little or absolutely no exposure to various media. The objective was to share HUL brand messages, to actively engage with consumers and to boost brand adoption metrics in rural markets.

The idea was to change the attitudes of the rural populace with regard to personal hygiene. The campaign aimed at inculcating good personal hygiene and enhancing preference for the company's brands by virtue of their association with daily hygiene habits. A multi-brand approach aimed at creating a cost efficient rural activation module, involving various personal care and home care brands of HUL like Surf Excel, Wheel, FAL, Vim, Lifebuoy, Sunsilk and Closeup. The module followed a 3-step process-awareness, consumer engagement and retail contact.

Over time, Unilever, a global conglomerate has pioneered a number of innovations that have helped sharpen its ability to cash in on rural market opportunities.

Its *Shakti* initiative is notable in this regard. It pioneered the concept of training local women as rural sales agents to sell Unilever products door to door in their communities. In 2015, the initiative was 70,000 sales agents strong and was serving 165,000 Indian villages. They had been equipped with Smartphone apps to manage inventory and other aspects of their business. Variations of the model were created in countries like Sri Lanka, Bangladesh,

Vietnam, Egypt, etc.

In Pakistan, Unilever gave this model an innovative twist by training hundreds of village women as beauticians, who followed the work from home model. They rolled out a three-month program in which the women, called Guddi Bajis, or "good sisters," were trained in the application of makeup, shampoo hair, and hw to provide other beauty services. This was in addition to learning how to sell Unilever products to their customers. This initiative empowered them with a dual income, for the beauty services they provided plus the commissions they earned on those sales as well as points toward incentives such as salon tables or mirrors.

The company soon realized the importance of religious congregations like the Kumbh Mela and took its marketing initiatives to millions of people who gathered there. In 2013, HUL and creative agency Ogilvy, partnered more than 100 *dhabas* and hotels at the *Kumbh Mela* site to serve rotis that were stamped with "*Lifebuoy se haath dhoye kya*?" (Have you washed your hand with Lifebuoy?). With a minimum of two people share a table, with this initiative HUL targetted much more than 2.5 million visitors at the *Maha Kumbh Mela*.

In 2019, Lifebuoy, the hygiene brand from Hindustan Unilever (HUL), served hygiene lessons to people through '*Swasthya Chetna Thalis*' at the ongoing *Kumbh Mela* at *Prayagraj*. The thalis came with an etched message of '*Kripaya Pehle Sabun se Haath Dhoyein*' ('Please wash your hands with soap first') reminding people to wash hands before eating. Their call to action spread the message that the simple act of washing hands can prevent many diseases that are caused by poor hand hygiene.

In this was HUL has introduced changes in its product, price, promotion and distribution strategies in sync with the unique characteristics of the rural markets in India.

2.2 Consumer Behaviour
2.2.1 Introduction
2.2.2 Meaning of Consumer Behaviour
2.2.3 Definition of Consumer
2.2.4 Scope of Consumer Behaviour
2.2.5 Determinants of Consumer Behaviour
2.2.6 Concept of Motivation
2.2.7 Theories of Motivation
2.2.8 Multivariable Models of Consumer Behaviour Behaviour
2.2.9 Buying Motives & Consumer Importance of Buying Motives
2.2.10 Monadic Models of Consumer
To develop the awareness amongst the students about how marketing strategy plays a vital role in making today's customers want to buy the products and services.

2.2.1 Introduction

Marketing revolves around a consumer and his/her needs. It is impossible for a company to cater to consumer needs without studying consumer behavior. All human behavior is driven by needs. People act in a certain manner in order to satisfy their needs and wants. Psychology studies human behavior and consumer behavior is a part of this vast subject.

Consumer behavioural studies help marketers to understand:

   1. What a consumer's needs and wants are?

2. What drives a consumer to buy products/services?

3. How, where and why consumers prefer to buy?

4. What makes consumers prefer a particular product/service over others?

5. How to market and promote products/services to consumers in general or a particular segment?

6. How to build brand loyalty?

7. What must be done to convert non users into users?

8. Profiling consumers.

Such information equips marketers with an understanding of what drives consumer behavior and enables the preparation of a marketing mix and marketing plan based on it.

2.2.2 Meaning of Consumer Behaviour

Consumer Behaviour is a decisional process and physical activity whereby consumers identify their needs and wants, search for products/services that will satisfy those needs and wants, evaluate alternatives, take the decision to buy a product, use it, experience it and if satisfied repeat the purchase. Thus, consumer behavior does not end with a purchase it comprises pre and post purchase behaviour. It comprises a study of the numerous influences on consumer behaviour across the spectrum of a wide range of subjects like economics, sociology, politics, psychology, and factors like lifestyle and trends. It refers to all the processes involved in the search, selection, consumption and post consumption decisions and influences on a consumer.

<u>**SOME DEFINITIONS**</u>

** Consumer Behaviour is the process whereby individuals decide what, when, where, how and from where to purchase goods and services. (Walters and Paul)*

** The dynamic interaction of cognition, behaviour and environmental events by which human beings conduct the exchange aspect of* *their lives. (The American Marketing Association)*

** Consumer Behaviour is "The mental and emotional processes and the observed behaviour during searching for, purchasing and post consumption of a product or service." (Engel, Blackwell and Miniard)*

** Consumer Behaviour refers to the actions and decision processes of people who purchase goods and services for personal consumption.*

(Peter D Bennet, ed. Dictionary of Marketing Terms, 2nd ed. 1995)

The following points highlight the nature of Consumer Behaviour and will help to further clarify the meaning of this concept:

1. Complex Nature: Consumer behaviour is rooted in psychology, the study of human behvaiour which is unpredictable. The behvaiour displayed by teenagers today is very different from the behaviour displayed by teenagers a decade or two decades ago. This is true across all age groups. For instance the Apple watch might look like a trendy gadget aimed at youth but it could find favour with senior citizens who live alone and need assistance with several tasks.

2. Varies across market segments: Depending on needs, desires, wants and purchasing power among many other factors, consumer behvaiour varies across different market segments. A service like education for toddlers, children, young adults, working professionals will be different. Or the type of car preferred by different consumers necessitates the Nexa (premium) range by Maruti Suzuki vis a vis their lower end buyers.

3. Dynamic Nature: Consumer Behaviour evolves in time. This is probably why there are people who look for vacations on Mars while others are heading to the rural hinterland to enjoy time off.

4. Influence: A Consumer's circle of family, friends, co-workers besides his/her lifestyle, aspirations, finances, place of residence, etc are just a few among the multiple factors that exert influence on his/her choices.

5. Important for Marketers: The study of consumer behvaiour is significant for marketers and advertisers. Marketing as a function, process and activity revolves around the consumer and all marketing plans and processes must be tuned into consumer needs, aspirations, wants and expectations.

6. Brand Loyalty: The concept of brand loyalty is rooted in consumer behaviour. Developing brand preference is possible only through in-depth understanding of consumer behaviour.

2.2.3 Definition of Consumer

The Oxford Dictionary defines a Consumer as "A person

who purchases goods and services for personal use"

The Merriam Webster Dictionary defines a Consumer as "one that utilizes economic goods"

Simply put a consumer is one who consumes a product/service or subscribes to an idea/school of thought. There is a difference between a buyer and a consumer. A buyer pays the price for a product/service; he may or may not consume what he has paid for. For example a parent pays the school fees of his child. Here the parent is the buyer and his child is the consumer of the service of education. If you buy a gift for someone, you are the buyer, the person who receives the gift from you could be the consumer provided he/she uses the item you gifted him/her. Thus the concept of consumer is rooted in utilization of a product/service,, not in the mere purchase.

2.2.4 Scope of Consumer Behaviour

Consumer Behaviour is a sub domain within the vast domain of psychology. Its scope includes the following disciplines:

1. **Economics:** Purchase is an economic decision which is taken by taking price considerations and forces of demand and supply into consideration. For instance, the recent lockdown imposed during the COVID-19 crisis fuelled greater

demand for groceries and items of necessity as people feared shortages. Had there been no apprehensions about scarcity the demand for groceries would have not gone up.

Demand forecasting is an intrinsic part of a firm's future planning and this demands the study of consumer behaviour. For instance it is being estimated that the COVID-19 crisis has compelled people to save for health reasons and to cushion themselves against the impact of salary cuts/job losses. Hence saving for education and weddings is not as much a priority as it used to be.

2. **Human Behaviour/Psychology:** Every consumer is a human being, driven by needs, wants, desires, aspirations and limited by lifestyle, culture, traditions, affordability, availability, etc. For instance a person who otherwise is thrifty and eats only healthy, home cooked food may be ready to spend an exorbitant amount on food and water when stranded at an airport simply because he is driven by his physiological needs as they are pre-dominant when one is hungry, tired, stranded and has no other alternative.

    If a buyer was considering the purchase of a car/bike before the COVID-19 crisis and his objective was to be independent and mobile now with lockdown restrictions in place the purchase will not take place because the need for mobility is relatively less/restricted. Thus consumer behaviour is situational/contextual and difficult to predict.

3. **Marketing:** Consumer Behaviour directs all marketing efforts of a firm because marketing begins with the study of consumer needs/wants. When McDonalds' came to India, it introduced the *Aloo Tikki* burger on its menu. This was necessary if it did not want to lose out catering to a large section of the Indian population which is vegetarian. Similarly the introduction of a Diet Coke or Diet Pepsi was driven by the need to cater to a growing number of consumers for whom health was a priority.

4. **Advertising:** Advertising is communication which aims at informing, educating and persuading consumers. In order to

create impactful advertising content and deliver it via suitable platforms a study of consumer behaviour is necessary. For instance increased mobile and internet penetration in India has necessitated advertising these media. Today even movies do not release without digital marketing campaigns. In depth study of consumer behaviour is the foundation on which good and relevant advertising campaigns catering to the needs of the target audience can be built.

The Scope of Consumer Behaviour from the perspective of a Process which is explained in the Consumer Motivation Theories in the EKB (Engel, Kollat and Blackwell)Model

2.2.5 Determinants of Consumer Behaviour

The determinants of Consumer Behaviour may be classified as follows:

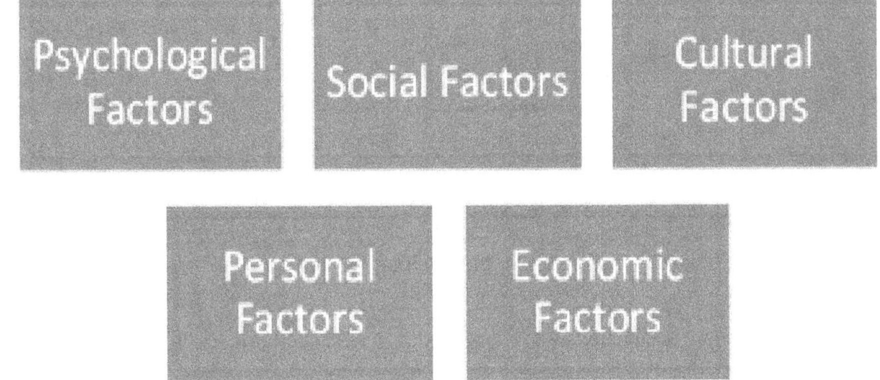

Psychological factors

Psychological factors include the following:

> Motivation
>
> Perception
>
> Learning
>
> Attitudes and Beliefs

1. **Motivation:** All human behaviour is need driven. People are motivated to act/speak/behave in a certain manner because they are driven by basic, social, economic, safety, prestige and self-actualization needs. Rational and emotional buying motives drive consumers to buy products/services.

2. **Perception:** It is the ability to see, hear, or become aware of something through the senses. It is also the way in which something is regarded, understood, or interpreted/

3. **Learning:** It *is* making sense or abstracting meaning. *Learning* involves relating parts of the subject matter to each other and to the real world. A lot of human behaviour is "learned" and so is the case with consumer behaviour. Oiling your hair gives strong, healthy hair this is something we are taught from childhood and that is what drives us to buy hair oil time and again. Eating almonds is good for health hence you buy almonds and so on.

4. **Attitudes and Beliefs:** Attitudes and beliefs are talked about as "things" or possessions individuals acquire in response to life experiences, personal values, and information from the social world. (From: Advances in Experimental Social Psychology, 2013).

Values are stable long-lasting beliefs held by people about what is important to them. They become standards by which people lead their lives and make their choices.

A belief develops into a value when the person's commitment to it grows and they see it as something important to live by. Beliefs can be classified into different types of values – such as values that relate to happiness, wealth, career success or family. A person should be able to articulate his/her values in order to make clear, rational, responsible and consistent decisions.

Attitudes are mental dispositions people have towards life, other people and current/future circumstances. Attitudes lead to decisions that result in behaviour. Attitudes are formed on the basis of underlying values and beliefs.

Social Factors

Reference Groups:

- Membership and Non-Memebership Groups
- Primary and Secondary Reference Groups

Roles and Status

- Position occupied by buyer in society/family/group

1. Reference Groups:

Reference Group is a group that serves as a reference point for an individual in the formation of his/her beliefs, attitudes and behaviour. The importance of reference groups in advertising is evident from how marketers advertise products in a group setting- the family eating breakfast together, watching a match with family/friends/ shopping together/ neighbors admiring a car/ even things like paint of the house. For instance Prestige has advertised its kitchenware with Abhishekh Bachchan and Aishwarya Rai Bachchan with the tagline *"jo biwi se kare pyar woh Prestige se kaise kare ink-*

aar?" for some time now.

Reference groups can be classified as membership and non-membership groups like family, friend circle, housing society (membership groups), etc and celebrities/influencers (non-membership groups). Family and people you interact with even at work on a day to day basis have the power to influence you and your buying behaviour. At the same time a celebrity or star is someone you might not interact with but could be your role model/s or someone you aspire to become/be like. Celebrity endorsements or even reviews by people who have bought a product on a shopping site (basically people you do not know) can influence consumer choices.

2. Role/Position

Role/Position Occupied in a group can impact Consumer Behaviour. Following are the 6 buying roles:

1. INITIATOR is the one who starts the buying process as he/she identifies the need to buy a particular product or service to solve an individual/organisational problem;
2. INFLUENCER his/her/their views influence the buyers and deciders/decision maker;
3. DECIDER usually the one who controls the finances or wields influence by virtue of his/her position in a group. The influencer ultimately approves all or any part of the entire buying decision -- whether to buy, what to buy, how to buy, and where to buy;
4. BUYER the person who pays for the product/service being purchased;
5. USER the person who is the ultimate user, he/she finally consumes or uses the product or service;
6. GATEKEEPER the person who controls information or access or both, to decision makers and influencers.

Cultural Factors

The cultural factors that impact consumer behaviour include:

1. Culture: Culture may be defined as the "personality of a society". It is comprehensive and includes language, customs and traditions, religion, norms and laws, art and music, etc. It also includes the attitudes, interests, opinions and values of people. It is reflected in the work practices and orientations people have as well as their approach towards general and specific issues. The do's and dont's of a society, all that is acceptable and all that is not is defined by Culture.

2. Sub-Culture: Culture is not entirely homogenous in nature. Within a social system it is possible that people do not share the same language, religion, customs and traditions. Every society comprises smaller sub-units that are homogenous within and heterogeneous outside. When put together they make a complex society. Such sub-units or sub-groups are known as sub-cultures; people within each sub-culture possess a distinctive set of values, beliefs, customs and traditions etc.

3. Social Class: Social class, also called class is a group of people within a society who share the same socio-economic status. Besides being important in social theory, the concept of class as a collection of individuals sharing similar economic circumstances is applicable to the decisions, choices and way of life adopted by that class.

Personal Factors

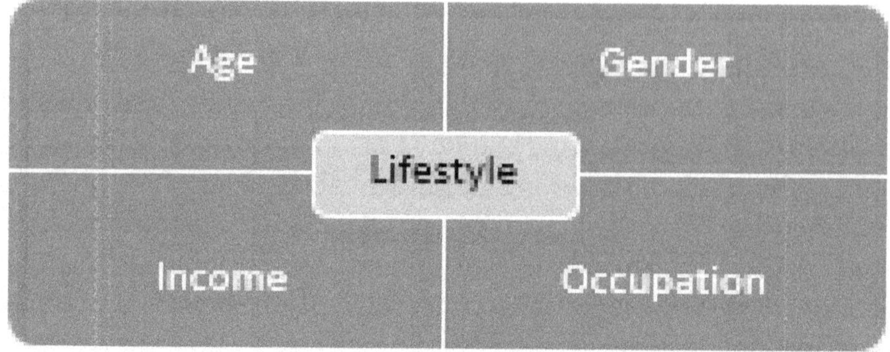

The personal factors impacting Consumer Behaviour can be broadly outlined below:

1. Age: Depending on age, consumer needs and requirements differ. Their behaviour will also differ based on their driving forces, attitudes, interests, lifestyle and so on.
2. Gender: This impacts the type of products /services used by consumers.
3. Income: Family and personal income define the purchasing power of consumers and accordingly impact the standadrd of living they enjoy/aspire to enjoy through the products/services they consume.
4. Occupation: The occupation of an individual dictates a lot of lifestyle choices and products/services consumed.
5. Lifestyle: This is how an individual spend his/her time. Lifestyle comprises a person's attitudes, interests, opinions and values.

2.2.6 Concept of Motivation:

The term **motivation** is derived from the word 'motive". **Motivation** may be defined as a planned managerial process, which stimulates people to work to the best of their capabilities, by providing them with motives, which are based on their unfulfilled needs. All human behaviour is driven by rational and/or emotional motives. An understanding of motivation helps marketers address consumer needs and requirements in a better manner.

Features of Motivation:

1. Psychological Process: Motivation is the reason for people's needs, behaviour, actions and choices.

2. Continuous Process: People are always engaged in seeking the satisfaction of one need after another. Some needs like the need for food, clothing and shelter are recurrent and have to be satisfied several times in a day or during a lifetime.

3. Goal Directed: Motivation is goal directed. People are always moving towards the attainment of a goal which could be described as fulfillment of various needs. For instance, goals such as financial independence or adequate returns on investment could lead people to invest in mutual funds.

4. Complex: Motivating people is complex because each person is different, his/her driving forces differ. Moreover driving forces are often contextual.

5. Influenced by Social and Cultural Norms: A person may be motivated to behave in a certain manner due to social/cultural norms. Vegetarianism may be a choice that is dictated by religion/the school of thought one subscribes to.

6. Is Positive and Negative: Motivation could be negative if you refrain from a certain thing. For instance negative motivation is amplified in advertisements that deter people from drinking and driving, domestic violence/cruelty to animals. Positive motivation is seen in advertisements that encourage people to eat right, exercise, educate the girl child, etc.

2.2.7 Theories of Consumer Motivation

Maslow's Need Hierarchy

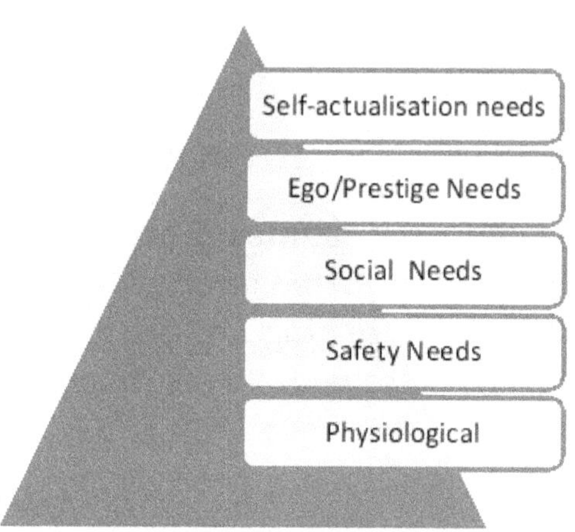

Abraham Maslow put forth the Theory of Hierarchy of needs in 1943. As per this theory, people are motivated to fulfill their needs based on a five-part priority system. The needs in order of importance are: physiological (survival), safety, love, esteem, and self-actualization.

Maslow's theory is widely accepted and applied in the domains of business and marketing to explain, understand and manage consumer behaviour. When applied by marketers to the study of Consumer behaviour, the effort is to determine where a product/service fits on the pyramid of hierarchy of needs. Consumers are motivated to prioritize purchases toward the base of the hierarchy in times of a crisis or shortages/adverse economic conditions but the same consumers will look at satisfying higher level needs when conditions are conducive.

The application of this theory works like this- during this pandemic, the need to re-skill has become obvious, hence spending on a car (prestige need) does not make sense but going back to studies and pursuing a new course to improve yourself (self-actualisation) makes a lot of sense.

Pavlov's Theory of Classical Conditioning

Ivan Pavlov, a Russian psychologist is best known for his work in classical conditioning. In 1904, his work in Classical Conditioning earned him the Nobel Prize in physiology or medicine.

Pavlov found that objects or events could trigger a conditioned response. He experimented by demonstrating how the presence of a bowl of dog food (stimulus) would trigger an unconditioned response (salivation). But Pavlov noticed that the dogs had begun to associate his lab assistant with food, thereby creating a learned and conditioned response. This was an important scientific discovery.

Pavlov then designed an experiment using a bell as a neutral stimulus. As he gave food to the dogs, he rang the bell. After repeating this procedure, he tried ringing the bell without giving any food to the dogs who salivated in anticipation of the food just by hearing the bell. The result of the experiment was a new conditioned response in the dogs.

Pavlov's theory later developed into the Classical Conditioning Theory, which refers to learning that associates an unconditioned stimulus that already results in a response (such as a reflex) with a new, conditioned stimulus. As a result, the new stimulus brings about the same response.

A simple application of Pavlovian theory is the response that some consumers have when they hear the word "sale." It can make them want to shop, even if they have no specific need at the time.

The theory can also work with specific brands. A consumer may start associating a brand name or product with a certain perception after repeated marketing efforts and/or experience with the brand or product. For instance, many people associate the brand name Dove with beauty and soft skin or Lux soap with beauty akin to that of film stars or Rooh Afza with refreshing, cool, rose flavoured drink.

Conditioning makes consumers conjure up images of health and fitness by just seeing the Nike Swoosh or a baby soft skin on seeing a Johnsons baby lotion even before using the product.

Theory of Reasoned Action

Propounded by Martin Fishbein and Icek Ajzen in the late 1960s, the Theory of Reasoned Action centers its analysis on the importance of pre-existing attitudes in the decision-making process. The core of the theory suggests that consumers act/ behave in a manner based on their intention to create or receive a particular outcome. According to this theory:

1. Consumers are rational beings who choose to act in their best interests and

2. Specificity is critical in the decision-making process.

A consumer only takes a specific action when an equally specific result is expected. From the time the consumer decides to act to the time the action is completed, the consumer retains the power/ability/freedom to change his or her mind and decide on a different course of action.

Marketers can gain from the application of Theory of Reasoned Action. First, when you market a product to consumers, you must associate a purchase with a specific and positive result. Fairness creams have done this for years, they link the use of the product to specific outcomes like fairness in 14 days/ ant acne creams work the same way-no pimples in 7 days/ anti aging creams/ anti dandruff and anti hair fall shampoos all work in the same way-they promise to give consumers positive and specific results.

However, just promising specific and positive results is not enough. A time lag between making the offer and closing the sale can give consumers time to change their mind. This is probably why a midnight sale for a day or an Independence Day sale might push people to buy more than a week or two week long sale.

Engel, Kollet, Blackwell (EKB) Model

The EKB Model further expands on the Theory of Reasoned Action. It defines a five-step process that consumers use when making a purchase.

Explained below 5 stages a consumer goes through as he/she arrives at a purchase decision:

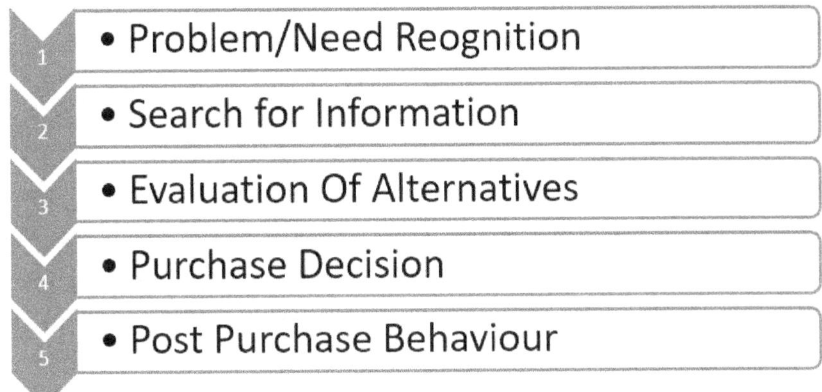

The process of Consumer Behaviour can be explained with the help of an example:

1. **Need/Problem Recognition:** This is the first step in the process. It is one in which the consumer experiences dissatisfaction about his/her situation or spots a gap between what he/she has and what he/she wants to have. A student who travels to college by bus has to spend a lot of time in the commute. Further crowded buses are a hotbed for infections and his health suffers a great deal on that account. Hence, he feels the need for his own vehicle which will function as his mode of transport. He realizes that this will save his time and the money he spends on doctor visits and medications for frequent infections/spells of illness.

2. **Search for Information:** This stage involves taking steps

to look for information about a suitable product/service which will fulfill/solve the need/problem identified. For this the following sources are tapped into:

Public and Commercial sources: Advertisements in newspapers, magazines, television, radio, promotional campaigns, sales people or product packaging.

Personal sources: The needs are discussed with family and friends who recommend products/services.

Experiential sources: First hand experience of users/buyers in the form of reviews and recommendations.

In the example stated in need recognition the student decides to look for information about suitable vehicles:

On tapping family and friends he understands that he could choose to cycle to college or buy a motorbike. His home is more than 5 kilometers away from his College and the route is congested and has heavy traffic hence a cycle might not be the safest option. Perhaps a bike or a lower priced car might be a good option. The car/bike thus purchased will be of use to others in his family. His parents will pay for the vehicle hence the decision regarding the purchase will be made by them. He looks for information on websites like cardekho, bikedekho and those of manufacturers and shares the same with his parents.

3. **Evaluation of Alternatives:** Once some alternative products/services are in mind the customer evaluates them on the basis of features, desirable attributes and cost-benefit analysis. In the example we have considered this might comprise an evaluation of a car/bike on the basis of design, fuel efficiency, price, reviews, maintenance/repair costs, ease of availability of spare parts, after sales service, schemes by banks for automobile loans, etc. To evaluate alternatives a test drive and visits to various showrooms may be undertaken.

4. **Purchase Decisions:** This involves making a choice-actively choosing one product/service over those available. At this

point all search and evaluation ends, action is taken by opting for a particular product/service. In the example-it would be actual purchase of a particular car or bike.

5. **Post Purchase Behaviour:** This is the experiential stage in which the consumer uses/consumes the product/service. He experiences satisfaction/dissatisfaction. If he is satisfied he will repeat the purchase or recommend the product/service to others. If he is dissatisfied he will do the opposite. In case of certain products post purchase behaviour will entail making use of after sales service like in case of the purchase of a vehicle in the example we have considered.

Under the EKB Model, there are 2 stages wherein input is the most valuable:

1. The initial information stage wherein marketers must provide consumers with enough information about the product to drive the consumer to keep the company's products under consideration for purchase.

2. Stage of external influences: wherein brands work on instilling a desire in the consumer to look or feel a certain way with the product, even if the brand/product/service is not fundamentally different from the competition.

Hawkins Stern Impulse Buying

While many of the theories of consumer behavior focus on rational action, the Hawkins Stern Model believes in the idea of impulse behavior. Stern contended that sudden purchase impulses fit alongside rational purchasing decisions to depict a true, fair and realistic picture of the average consumer. Impulse purchases are largely driven by external stimuli and have almost no relationship to traditional decision-making.

Stern established four categories of impulse buying:

1. Pure impulse purchases: like picking up chocolates at the checkout line of a grocery store.

2. Reminded impulse buys: like placing a display of salad dips next to a display of fresh vegetables or freshly packed salad fruit/vegetables.

3. Suggested impulse purchases: such as an extended warranty for an electronic device/ servicing of automobile.

4. Planned impulse decisions: where consumers know they want to buy a product, but are unsure about the specifications.

This theory moves away from the sheer "rationality" of purchases and shows that impulse buying is a significant part of consumer behaviour. Impulse buying theories open up endless possibilities for marketers. From product display to packaging everything has the power to trigger impulse buying and this knowledge can equip marketers to influence consumers towards purchases. Marketers can use appropriate strategies to engage with customers and close the sale.

Nicosia Model of Consumer Behavior was developed in 1966, by Professor Francesco M. Nicosia, an expert in consumer motivation and behavior. This model focuses on the relationship between the firm and its potential consumers. The model suggests that messages from the firm (advertisements) first influences the predisposition of the consumer towards the product or service. Based on the situation, the consumer will have a certain attitude towards the product. This may result in a search for the product or an evaluation of the product attributes by the consumer. If the above step satisfies the consumer, it may result in a positive response, with a decision to buy the product otherwise the reverse may occur. Looking to the model we will find that the firm and the consumer are connected with each other, the firm tries to influence the consumer and the consumer is influencing the firm by his decision.

The **Nicosia model of Consumer Behavior** is divided into four major fields:

1. **Field 1: The firm's attributes and the consumer's attributes.** The first field is divided into two subfields. The first subfield deals with the firm's marketing environment and communication efforts that affect consumer attitudes, the competitive environment, and characteristics of target market. Subfield two specifies the consumer characteristics e.g., experience, personality, and how he perceives the promotional idea toward the product in this stage the consumer forms his attitude toward the firm's product based on his interpretation of the message.

2. **Field 2: Search and evaluation.** The consumer will start to search for other firm's brand and evaluate the firm's brand in comparison with alternate brands. In this case the firm motivates the consumer to purchase its brands.

3. **Field 3: The act of the purchase.** The result of motivation will arise by convincing the consumer to purchase the firm products from a specific retailer.

4. **Field 4: Feed back of sales results.** This model analyses the feedback of both the firm and the consumer after purchasing the product. The firm will benefit from its sales data as a feedback, and the consumer will use his experience with the product affects the individuals attitude and predisposition's concerning future messages from the firm.

2.2.8 Multivariable Models of Consumer Behaviour

Economic Man Model

In this model, consumers follow the principle of maximum utility based on the law of diminishing marginal utility. Economic man model is based on 3 effects –

- **Price Effect** – Lower the price of the product higher will be the quantity purchase.

- **Substitution Effect** – Lower the price of the substitute product, lower will be the utility of the original product purchase.

- **Income Effect** –In case of more income/more availability of money, higher quantity will be purchased.

The economic theory of buyer's decision-making was based on the following assumptions –

1. As a consumer has limited resources, he will allocate the amount available so as to maximize the satisfaction of his needs and wants.

2. Consumers have complete knowledge about the utility of each product and service, i.e., they are capable of determining the amount of satisfaction that each item they purchase is likely to produce.

3. According to the Law of Diminishing Marginal Utility, when more units of the same item are purchased the marginal utility or satisfaction derived from the next unit of the item will keep on decreasing, according to the law of diminishing marginal utility.

4. Price is used as a measure of sacrifice in obtaining products/services.

5. A buyer's overall objective is to derive maximum satisfaction from the act of purchase.

Learning Model

The Learning Model suggests that human behavior is based on some core concepts – the drives, stimuli, cues, responses and re-inforcements which determine the human needs and wants and needs satisfying behavior.

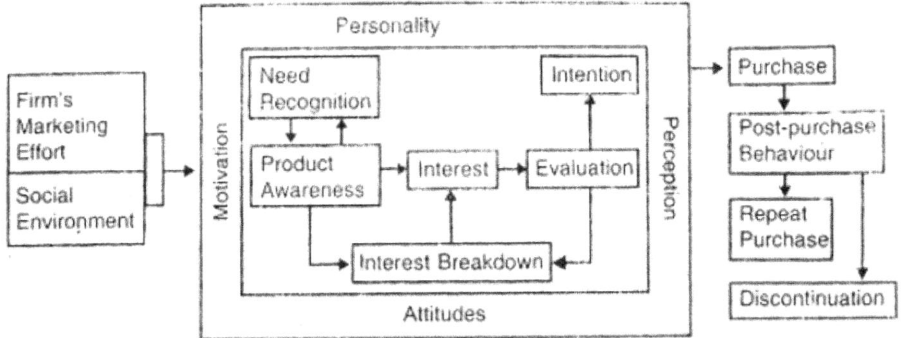

• **Drive** – A strong internal stimulus which compels action.

• **Stimuli** – Inputs capable of arousing drives or motives.

• **Cues** – A sign or signal which acts as a stimulus to a particular drive.

• **Response** – How an individual reacts to stimuli.

If the response to a certain stimulus is "rewarding", it reinforces the possibility of similar response when faced with the same stimulus or cues. For instance if an informational cue like advertising/recommendation by an influencer spurs purchase (response), a favourable experience with the product increases the probability that the response would be repeated the next time the need stimulus arises (reinforcement).

Psychoanalytic Models

1. Freud's Psychoanalytic Model

Proposed by Sigmund Freud, the model tries to explain consumer behavior as a result of forces that operate at subconscious level. According to the model, consumer needs and desires operate at multiple levels of consciousness. Not all behavior is understandable and explainable nor overtly visible and explainable. Sometimes, people may not realise and understand what causes/prompts his own behaviour. Such causes can be understood by drawing inferences from observation and casual probing. Every consumer has a set of deeply rooted motives which drive him to take certain purchase decisions.

2. Gestalt model

The model based on Gestalt principles (meaning "patterns and configuration") gives importance to the perceptual processes that impact buying behavior. According to this model, consumption behavior and decision making is based on how a consumer perceives a stimuli. Such as the Marketing Mix vis a vis. the external environment and the consumer's prior experiences.

3. Cognitive Model

Proposed by Leon Festinger, this model views the consumer as one who experiences anxiety (dissonance), while making a purchase. This is because he is faced with many alternatives/choices, all of which seem desirable/attractive. Post-purchase, this dissonance increases even further. There is an imbalance in the cognitive structure; and the consumer tries to get out of this state as soon as he can. Hence, a buyer gathers information to support his choice and avoids information that goes against it.

Sociological Model

This model is concerned with society. A consumer is part of society and he may be a member of many groups and institutions within society. His buying behavior is influenced by these groups. As a member of an elite organization, his dress needs may be different, thus he has to buy things that confirm to his lifestyle in different groups. This part has been explained in reference groups under determinnats of buyer behaviour earlier in the chapter.

2.2.9 Buying Motives & Importance of Consumer Buying Motives

Let us understand what a motive is. "A motive is the inner state that moves, or prompts a person to action."

What is a Buying Motive?
"A motive may be defined as a drive or an urge for which can individual seeks satisfaction. It becomes a buying motive when the individual seeks satisfaction through the purchase of something." (W. J. Stanton)
"Buying motives are those influences or considerations which provide the impulse to buy, induce action or determine choice in the purchase of goods and services." (D. J. Durdian)

Types of Buying Motives:

- **Physical, Psychological and Sociological Buying Motives:**

The psychological buying motives are related to the satisfaction of basic human needs for subsistence ie. food, clothing, shelter and security.

Psychological buying motives relate to the need for prestige or self-preservation/self-importance, etc.

Sociological buying motives are related to the motives existing/likely to arise in all the social situations.

- **Acquired and Inherent Buying Motives:**

Acquired buying motives are learned and arise due to the impact of environmental factors. The need to be beautiful, fairer, fashionable etc arise due to external influences/comparison/social pressures.

Inherent buying motives are inborn and arise from human instincts. Hunger, thirst, sleep, leisure, relaxation are all spurred by instinct.

- **Primary and Selective Buying Motives**

Primary buying motives relate to general needs like that for a car, bike, mobile phone, television, etc. Selective buying motives relate to preference for specific brands like that for a Samsung mobile phone, Sony TV, Hero Honda bike, Mercedes Benz car, etc.

- **Conscious and Dormant Buying Motives**

Conscious Buying Motives are those motives which a consumer does not need any external influences to make him aware of. Conscious buying motives relate to things like hunger/ thirst. Dormant Buying Motives are those which require external influences to generate awareness in a consumer. For instance a customer starts craving chocolates when he sees them on display at the checkout counter of a grocery store.

- **Rational and Emotional Buying Motives**

Rational motives are driven by logic and reasoning. Consumers may buy products due to reasonable price, convenience, ease of use, after sales service when they make rational choices.

Emotional buying motives are related to feelings and emotions. Consumers buy expensive gifts as a token of love/ insurance to protect their family/care for a loved one. Such purchases are driven by emotions.

- **Product and Patronage Buying Motives**

Where a consumer buys a product due to its features, specifications, price, he is driven by product buying motives. A graphic designer chooses to buy a laptop based on its graphics card, user interface, memory specifics; etc is driven by a product buying motive.

Patronage Buying Motive refers to instances where consumers are driven by loyalty to a particular product/store/organisation. For instance a family that purchases a Tata Motors automobile each time is driven by Patronage.

Various scholars have classified buying motives as:

E.J. McCarthy:

1. Satisfaction of senses, 2. Preservation of Species, 3. Fear, 4. Pride, 5. Sociability, 6. Striving, 7. Curiosity, 8. Rest and Recreation.

Charles.B.Roth

1. Hunger, 2. Nature, 3. Fear, 4. Sex, 5. Jealousy, 6. Envy, 7. Conflict, 8. Social Impression, 9. Curiosity. 10. Love, 11. Pride, 12. Relaxation, 13. Greed, 14. Personal Proress, etc are main motives.

Melvin. S. Hattwick

He has broadly classified motives as Primary and Secondary Buying Motives. Primary motives are inherent and secondary motives are acquired.

Importance of Buying Motives:
1. A good understanding of buyer motives facilitates better marketing initiatives/planning/formulation of the marketing mix to induce customers to buy products/services
2. Aids salesmen in serving the customer according to his driving forces/motives.
3. Facilitates the formulation of appropriate pricing policies/discounts/offers.
4. Empowers firms to package, present and place the product effectively.
5. Facilitates the identification of the most suitable distribution channels, logistics and delivery mechanisms that will reach the target audience with ease and efficiency.
6. Helps in devising promotional plans and materials to influence consumers in the most appropriate manner.
7. Due to attention to consumer buying motives helps firm to earn goodwill in the market.

CASE STUDY: TTK's PRESTIGE

The TTK Prestige group, incorporated in 1955 started manufacturing. Pressure cookers in 1959 with technical collaboration from the **Prestige** Group of the United Kingdom. The brand had the challenge of dealing with its target audience-the Indian housewife who was familiar with traditional cooking techniques and uninitiated in the use of time saving gadgets like the pressure cooker. The primary concern for Indian housewives at the time was safety while cooking. Prestige focused on giving women safe cooking solutions. Its innovations like the pressure release valve made the prestige Pressure Cocker stand out as a safe appliance. Circa 1982, Those were the days when one heard of pressure cookers exploding in kitchens. Prestige's arch rival at that that time was Hawkins which was ruling the roost.

Against this backdrop Prestige came out with their TVC starring Raja Bundela who visits a kitchen appliances store to buy a pressure cooker where the cheeky shopkeeper asks him-how much do you love your wife-this seemed like a nosy almost outrageous question but as the ad unfolded the narrative shifted to the gasket release system of the Prestige pressure cooker –high level safety for a wife from a her husband who loves her more than life itself. The iconic tagline "Jo Biwi se kare pya who prestige se kaise kare inkaar-" which translates as "If you love our wife, you will not refuse to buy Prestige" was penned by Sadiqa Peerbhoy of Bangalore-based MAA ad agency. The ad film was an apt conveyor of emotions attaching much significance to a husband-wife relationship, it turned the tide for many in the business, it was directed by noted ad man, Prahlad Kakkar for MAA.

Apart from the Pressure Cooker, the Prestige Pressure Pan was another invention that added ease and safety to the Indian kitchen.

In the early to mid 2000, Prestige realized that more and more women were stepping out of their homes to work, but their responsibility of cooking at home remained. This meant that women had additional responsibilities and there was a need to invent products that saved time so that women could be more productive in less time.

This led to the launch of a new smart range of innovative cooking and kitchen products under the umbrella of a new communication campaign titled 'Are you ready for a smarter kitchen?'.

By 2008, continuous inventions ensured that Prestige had covered all requirements of the modern Indian Kitchen. Their products were widely appreciated and Prestige had grown beyond the safest Pressure Cooker tp a 'Total Kitchen Solutions' provider.

Alongside this reinvention, Prestige had expanded into the retail network arena to ensure that the brand could connect with customers in a direct interface through the Prestige SmartKitchen stores they established pan India. .

The year 2013 saw Prestige scaling new heights on many fronts. They achieved phenomenal growth in the retail network touching the mark of 500 Prestige Xclusive Retail outlets across India.

The demand for Microwave Cookers was growing worldwide, and Prestige decided to cash in on the opportunity/ They launched the Prestige Microwave cookers and their product was well received in the Export market, the company saw a gross turnover of Rs 13.8 Billion (28% CAGR in 10 years).

The same year Prestige took on the Iconic B-town couple Aishwarya Rai and Abhishek Bachan as brand ambassadors. The campaign directed by Amit Sharma - one of industry's best and conceptualized by DDB Mudra was a definitive move by Prestige to differentiate itself from other kitchen appliance brands. They added the glam quotient to the campaign which represented the true spirit of 'Simmering love, togetherness. The comprehensive print and digital campaign featured six new TV commercials and aimed at modern day consumers. The transition from a safe brand to a reliable, robust and innovative brand that celebrates conversations, camaraderie and contemporary style slowly became evident in the brand's journey.

In 2015, Prestige stretched their limits and got back to double-digit growth in most difficult circumstances which led to an increase in market share across categories and they crossed 15 Billion milestone in turnover.
In 2016, Prestige entered into a new horizon with UK Acquisition, they also launched Cleaning Solutions to reduce the burden

of daily chores on a housewife.

In 2017, Prestige launched the 'Judge' brand to reach out a larger customer base. They also launched gravity based Tattva range of water purifiers with Copper storage container and advanced FACT filters to facilitate chemical-free water purification method. Thereby catering to different price points and adding to their product offerings.

In 2018, Prestige moved beyond Kitchen Domain to adopt an aggressive long range plan- to simplify offerings to suit the needs of the contemporary customer with a wide range of kitchen cookware and appliances. They sought to become more relevant and widened their customer base. This was reflected in the tweak to their tagline which evolved to become "Joh apnon se kare pyar, woh prestige se kaise kare inkaar". They took on cine star, Vidya Balan as their brand ambassador. This association commenced with a national brand campaign that ran to the end of April on all media platforms which included but was not limited to TV, print and digital. This new celebrity brand ambassador and diversification into the Prestige Clean Home was an endeavour to establish a meaningful connect with the modern Indian home-maker, their core audience.

CHAPTER 3:
MARKETING PLANNING

3.1 Introduction
3.2 Meaning of Marketing Planning
3.3 Definition of Marketing Planning
3.4 Nature of Marketing Planning
3.5 Scope of Marketing Planning
3.6 Elements of Marketing Planning
3.7 Importance of Marketing Planning
3.8 Types of Marketing Planning

3.1 Introduction

Nothing in life can be achieved without planning and in business the need and importance of planning is manifold. Marketing planning is instrumental at different stages in the life of a product/brand/service/company/institution. The objective could be launching/introducing a new product/service/variant or reviving a dying brand.

3.2 Meaning of Marketing Planning

Planning is the backdrop for any activity/process. It involves taking stock of where one is right now and where one wants to be in future. Planning addresses this gap-between where you are and where you want to be. To put is simply, Marketing planning is the backdrop against which any business enterprise functions. Marketing planning is the process which helps a business to bridge the gap between its future marketing goals and objectives and current status as far as its market share, sales, distribution, number of products/range of products, etc go.

The process involves forecasting, exploring possible courses of actions/decisions, anticipating consequences, predicting the outcome of such events and decisions, all of which must be carried out while evaluating internal resources and capabilities and dynamism of the external environment in which a business functions. No business functions in a vacuum and must consider its competitors, customers, changing trends, socio-economic, political and cultural factors while planning.

Marketing planning like any form of planning is future oriented. It is always carried out in the light of marketing objectives which may be different for each firm- survival, growth, profit maximization, cost leadership, maintaining status-quo, etc. In case of Maggi noodles their marketing objectives immediately after the ban in 2015 were restoring customer faith, post re-launch it was reclaiming market share, building customer confidence, ensuring availability of the product and thereafter the objectives became product diversification to reduce over dependence on Maggi noodles.

Marketing planning essentially involves preparation of a marketing plan which is the foundation of a firm's marketing efforts. It outlines objectives and the resources that must be employed to achieve them.

A marketing plan is a written document that outlines the future course of action which a firm must take to meet its marketing objectives.

3.3 Definition of Marketing Planning

Marketing Planning is a systematic process involving the assessment of marketing opportunities and resources, the determination of marketing objectives and the development of a plan for implementation and control

(Kotler on Marketing, 1999)

From Philip Kotler's definition of marketing planning we can understand that it is **an analytical process** that involves taking stock of the **current situation.** It is a **forward looking process** that establishes some goals/objectives to be achieved ahead. It is a **predictive function** that requires the firm to prepare forecasts and estimates. It is **strategic in nature** because it involves decisions relating to the best possible use of available resources to achieve marketing objectives while taking the external and internal environment into consideration.

Marketing Planning is the work of setting up objectives

for marketing planning activity and of determining and scheduling the steps necessary to achieve such objectives. (The American Marketing association)

The definition of marketing planning put forth by the AMA highlights the goal oriented nature of marketing planning. It also gives readers an idea about the steps involved in the process of marketing planning i.e. establishing/defining objectives followed by outlining and scheduling the activities that must be performed in order to achieve those objectives.

Marketing Planning is the logical sequence of activities leading to the setting of marketing objectives and formulation of plans for achieving them. (MalColm.H.B. Mc Donald)

The definition by MalColm. H. B. Mc Donald indicates that marketing planning is a process/sequence of activities whereby objectives are defined and plans prepared to meet those objectives.

Marketing Planning is the exercise of analysis and foresight to increase the effectiveness of marketing activities. (Wendell. R. Smith)

Wendell. R. Smith presents marketing planning as an "exercise" which could be construed as an activity as well as the use/application of analysis and a forward looking approach with the objective of enhancing the overall effectiveness of marketing endeavors.

3.4 Nature of Marketing Planning:

Marketing Planning is a managerial function that requires persons performing it to expend mental energy. The definitions of Marketing Planning discussed above clearly indicate its nature as:

1. An Analytical Process: Marketing Planning is contextual. Its effectiveness and success depends upon the analysis of the situation or environment (internal and external). For instance the launch of the iPhone 11 Pro with 3 cameras is a product feature which is directly related to the changing use of a phone for photography. With this feature Apple has given mobile phone users greater creative control over the photos they take. In the process it also established a benchmark for its competitors and changed the landscape for mobile phone marketing.

2. Future Oriented: Marketing Planning involves looking ahead. It involves a careful assessment of future opportunities and threats and the preparation of long term and short term plans. It is deciding in advance as to what to do at a future date. In the context of the complete ban which Maggi noodles faced in 2015, their short term plan involved making a comeback, medium term plan involved reclaiming market share and restoring consumer confidence while their long term plan included product diversification to reduce dependence on Maggi noodles as their top revenue grosser.

3. Goal Oriented: Goals/objectives are the guiding light of marketing planning. It involves the determination of objectives and goals in the light of the future conditions, trends, developments and environmental forces. These conditions may be conducive or otherwise and marketing planning is necessary to prepare for the opportunities/challenges they present. For instance the creation of Voice Assistants like Alexa, Google Assistant and Siri help automate life's little choices. They are boon considering how busy lives are and will most likely get even busier in future. Such products help in markets where there is a large/growing aging population. They are a good example of a future oriented approach by

Amazon, Google and Apple respectively.

4. Competitive in Context: The importance of competition in the context of a marketing plan cannot be overemphasized. In the absence of competition, marketing plans would not be necessary simply because a firm would have nothing to outdo or better itself against other than its own past performance. If you have ever heard Steve Jobs launching a product you will realize how the context of each product whether it was the MacBook or the iPhone or any other product he was launching, was always the competition. He highlighted the features of existing electronic devices and showed how Apple made their products several notches higher/more advanced and user friendly. That is ingenuity in marketing.

5. Strategic in Approach: Marketing Planning involves the selection of the best course of action from among the alternatives available. What is the best course of action for one company need not be what is best for another. A strategic approach will also involve opting for the most affordable and effective way to reach marketing goals/objectives. For instance when Hector Beverages launched Paper Boat, they were competing with cola majors. They were innovative not only about their products and packaging but also about their marketing initiatives. For nearly two years the brand stuck to digital platforms like Facebook to engage with customers and promote their offerings. As a nascent brand the budgets for television campaigns were comparatively huge and digital platforms and creative initiatives gave paper Boat a wider reach and greater engagement.

6. Complexity: Marketing Planning is a complex process. Defining the correct goals/objectives and making appropriate plans to achieve them is not an easy task. Strong analytical skills, adequate, complete and relevant information about various controllable and uncontrollable factors is what makes it a complex process. Balancing resources and goals in the midst of a fluid environment is the tightrope walk every firm must walk.

7. Dynamic: Marketing Planning is a dynamic process. This is due to the ever changing and transient nature of consumer behavior, competition, trends and economic cycles all of which are beyond the control of a firm. The best example of firms operating in a highly dynamic environment and responding to it is that of mobile phone manufacturers. Due to the sheer frequency with which tech geeks and people who view mobile phones as style statements change handsets, companies are always on their toes and release new models at regular intervals.

Another really good example of the dynamism of the environment is that of the COVID-19 crisis. Most businesses were taken completely unawares by it and its impact. The tourism and hotel industry has experienced unprecedented turmoil and losses due to it. Some shocks like these are completely unexpected and devastating. No amount of planning could have foreseen the upheaval caused by this crisis.

8. Formal and Corrective: Marketing planning is a very formal and corrective process. For instance the introduction of the Swiggy Genie service to ship parcels and ferry groceries during the lockdown was a formal and corrective marketing move by Swiggy, an on demand food delivery service. The need of the hour for many people during these lock downs was home delivery of groceries. Swiggy did not stop food delivery but just adapted to the possibility that demand for food deliveries might dip and demand for a service like Genie might surge. Thus, it did not insist on being a specialist and made room for a service which was not its forte' but the need of the hour. Such corrective measures help to keep the revenue coming in.

9. Decisive and Preventive: Marketing planning is a decisive activity because it involves choosing the most appropriate course of action from the many available. It is preventive in nature as it seeks to minimize/eliminate losses and reduce the impact that sudden/predicted changes can induce.

10. Optimistic and Pessimistic: It is an activity that compels firms to look ahead with hope for the future. At the same time it predicts problems/difficulties/adversities for the business and as such looks on the downside. In a way Marketing planning is about optimism and pessimism.

3.5 Scope of Marketing Planning

1. Marketing Objectives:

Marketing objectives are goals defined by a brand/company. Such defined goals provide clear and necessary direction for the company and its employees to work towards. A periodic review of these goals is necessary to ensure that they stay relevant and are redefined if necessary. These goals are an essential part of the marketing strategy.

The establishment of clear marketing objectives equips the marketing department and executives with the required information to achieve definite targets.

2. Marketing strategies and tactics: A *marketing strategy* is a firms' competitive plan, a well defined road-map. Whereas marketing tactics are strategic actions that direct the promotion of products/services to achieve specific marketing goals.

Marketing Strategy can be described as the general direction set for the company and its various components to achieve a desired state in the future. A marketing strategy results from a detailed strategic planning process.

A marketing strategy integrates marketing activities to utilize and allocate scarce resources so as to meet the present objectives.

Let us understand Marketing Strategy with the example of Reliance which launched Jio in 2016. They had one of the best customer acquisition plans. They offered free services to all their users for 3-6 months to all their users. They were able to gain over 16 million subscribers within the first month of their launch.

Their pricing strategy was another reason why they were able to make inroads into a highly competitive market. Jio started with a plan of INR 149 where the customers got:

- Unlimited texts, local or STD
- High-speed internet 4G usage
- Students get an additional 25% off on data usage if their registration is done on their student ID.

3. Marketing activities: *Marketing activities* comprise all the activities a firm performs to achieve its marketing goals. This includes: branding, packaging, pricing, advertising, sales promotion and physical distribution. The efficacy of these activities is enhanced by good marketing planning and research.

4. Marketing costs: Marketing cost is the total **cost** associated with delivering goods or services to customers. **Marketing cost** may comprise expenses incurred to store, promote, distribute and transfer the title of goods to a customer. In the context of banks, running an ATM (Automated Teller Machine) and maintenance of websites for net banking, phone banking, customer support are all part of marketing costs incurred by them.

5. Projected Results: *The desired and optimum results in marketing* are the smaller metrics that make up a *marketing campaign*. In case of the Reliance Jio launch mentioned above the 16 million subscribers acquired in the first month are the results they obtained. Such tangible results indicate what a company has gained with its marketing budget.

The marketing ROI (Return on Investment) is a popular metric which firms use to measure results. Apart from this here are many new technology-based marketing programs and tools with which marketer's abilities to capture data and evaluate results in quantitative terms are enhanced.

3.6 Elements of Marketing Planning

Marketing Planning comprises four fundamental elements. It would be pertinent to mention that these elements are not exclusive to marketing planning but extend to the overall planning function:

1. Objectives.

Objectives are definitive statements of future conditions expressed in quantitative and qualitative terms. Objectives/goals represent future achievements. The important of SMART goals has been discussed by many management thinkers and authors, SMART goals are specific, measurable, achievable, relevant and time bound. Successful planning demands the prioritization of objectives, defining the time frame for the achievements and parameters to measure the same. Example of a marketing objective: 5% increase in sales or 20% increase in market share.

Areas in which quantification of measurement of objectives is needed:
market standing
innovations
productivity
physical and financial resources
 profitability
 manager performance and responsibility
worker performance and attitude
social responsibility.
(Peter Drucker)

2. Programmes:

A programme refers to the detailed part of a marketing plan. It is our plan of action. It points out the responsibilities of each department involved in marketing effort. It outlines the steps to be taken by each department to achieve established goals within a specified period.

For instance the goal of increasing sales/expanding market share will have programmes for new product design and development, advertising, sales promotion, pricing and distribution.

3. Schedule: A schedule is a time-bound plan of action. Definite time lines are necessary to ensure the completion of all tasks necessary to achieve goals/objectives.

4. A budget is a financial plan. It is a document indicating the amount of resources allotted for a specific pur¬pose or work in an organisation. A marketing budget indicates estimated amounts which can be spent for financing all marketing activities in order to achieve pre-determined goals. Quantity, quality, time and cost are the standards established to measure of results.

3.7 Importance of Marketing Planning

The **benefits** of planning include (from McDonald, Marketing Plans, 1999):

- To help identify sources of competitive advantage
- To force an organized approach
- To ensure consistent relationships
- To inform
- To get resources
- To get support
- To gain commitment
- To set objectives and strategies
- To spell out the desired mix of products and services

As an activity that determines the goals/objectives and future course of action of a company Marketing Planning is of immense importance for any company that wants to succeed. Its significance for a firm may be explained as follows:

1. Insulation against Future Uncertainties:

Marketing planning is future oriented. It takes into account possible risks and uncertainties. This analysis is carried out based on current trends and projections for the future. Not all risks and events occurring in future can be predicted. For instance the unprecedented, devastation caused by natural disasters, war/political tensions/health crises like the COVID-19 crisis. However planning helps firms to prepare for risks arising out of competition in their domain, slow economic growth, possible reduction in demand, etc.

2. Provision of Direction /Focus to Marketing Activities

Marketing Planning enables a firm to carry out its marketing activities in a focused manner. This is evident from the Nestle Maggi Noodles case study cited at the beginning of the chapter. Their immediate focus was to make a comeback and restore confidence while their plans for the long term were reducing dependence on Maggi Noodles and product diversification.

3. Taking Advantage of Opportunities:

The future may be full of challenges but it also filled with many possibilities and opportunities. In case of Maggi noodles loss of trust/confidence was the challenge, it still is even 5 years down the line but these challenges hold within them seeds of opportunities to diversify and strengthen the brand portfolio. A robust planning system helps a firm to monitor the environment regularly and identify opportunities to cash in on.

4. Developing the Right Marketing Mix:

The marketing mix is a set of controllable variables and their levels that a firm uses to influence its target market. The product/service/idea is at the core of this and it comprises elements such as price, promotion, physical distribution, people, process and physical evidence. All these elements are combined in the right proportion to achieve a firm's marketing objectives.

5. Better Coordination and Control:

Marketing plans are aligned with the overall objectives and plans of the organisation. This facilitates the coordination of all marketing activities with those of the entire organisation.

6. Customer Satisfaction:

Customer satisfaction is the primary goal of any commercial organisation. Marketing planning enables a firm to achieve this through a study of customer needs, wants and expectations, guiding product development, pricing, promotion and distribution accordingly.

7.Economizing Operations: Marketing planning equips a firm with the information it requires to function an economical and effective manner. It facilitates optimum and judicious utilization of resources.

3.8 Types of Marketing Planning

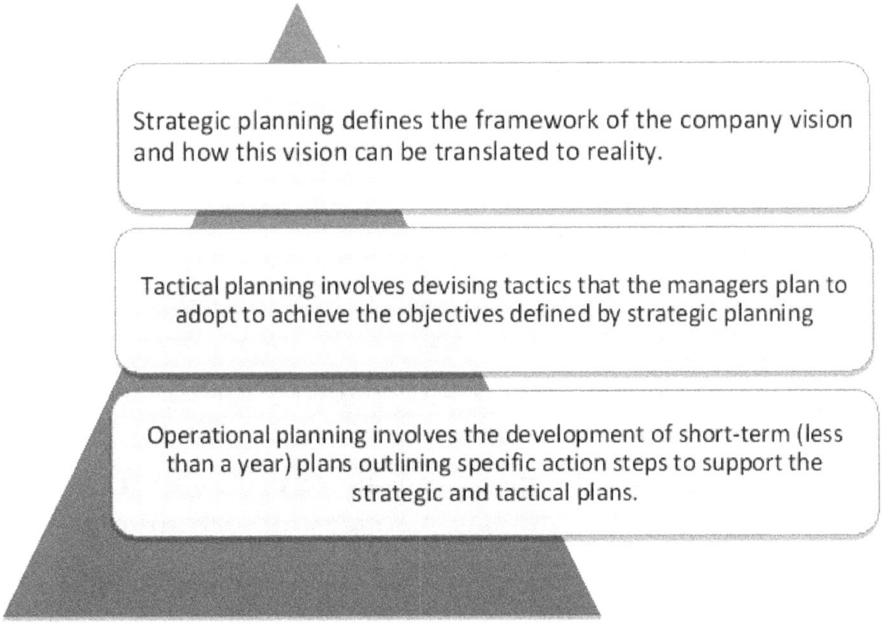

Strategic planning defines the framework of the company vision and how this vision can be translated to reality.

Tactical planning involves devising tactics that the managers plan to adopt to achieve the objectives defined by strategic planning

Operational planning involves the development of short-term (less than a year) plans outlining specific action steps to support the strategic and tactical plans.

Figure: 3.1 The hierarchy of Marketing Planning/plans

Types of Marketing Planning can be explained as follows:

1.   Strategic Planning

Strategic planning defines the framework of the company's marketing vision and how this vision can be translated to reality.

- It involves the determination of long-term enterprise marketing and overall objectives of an enterprise, the plan of action to be implemented and the resources to be mobilized to achieve these objectives.

- It is planning the overall direction of company progress and is done by the top management of an organization.

- Its focus is on planning for the coming years to take the organization from where it stands today to where it wants to be in future.

- Strategic planning must be forward looking, effective and flexible, with a focus on accommodating future growth.

· It provides the basis, framework and direction for lower level planning.

2. Tactical Planning

Tactical planning involves devising marketing tactics that the managers plan to adopt to achieve the objectives defined by strategic planning

· Tactical planning relates to a short term planning for a period usually less than 3 years).

· Tactical planning is carried out by middle level managers.

· It outlines the specific means or plan of action to implement the strategic plan by units within each division.

· Tactical planning involves outlining details of resource and work allocation among the subunits within each division of the organisation.

Operational Planning

Operational planning involves the development of short-term (less than a year) marketing plans outlining specific action steps to support the strategic and tactical plans.

· Operational plans are typically prepared by the concerned manager to fulfill his or her job responsibilities.

· Such plans are developed by supervisors, team leaders, and facilitators to support tactical plans.

· They govern the day-to-day operations of an organization.

· Operational plans are either –

   · **Standing plans** – Drawn up to cover issues managers face repeatedly, e.g. policies, procedures, rules.

   · **Ongoing plans** – Prepared for single or exceptional situations or problems and are normally discarded or replaced after one use, e.g. programs, projects, and budgets.

Another significant type of Marketing planning that does not fit into the above hierarchy is Planning for Contingencies

Contingency planning is devising plans for sudden/ unexpected/ unforeseen changes/developments occur or major changes/adjustments must be made in order to continue in the direction of achieving the organisational goals. Good contingency plans often are the difference between business success/failure. All changes cannot be predicted hence the importance of contingency planning for an organisation cannot be overemphasized. The example of the Swiggy Genie explained earlier in this book is the perfect example of a Contingency Plan.

3.9 Principles behind Successful Planning

1. Principle of Commitment:

The achievement of marketing objectives demands commitment of various resources. This satisfies the purpose of planning.

2. Principle of the Limiting Factor:

The importance of various factors comprising a plan is different. Further some of these factors may be rare/scarce/limited/expensive. Highlighting such factors is necessary to select the most favorable alternative.

3. Principle of Reflective Thinking:

Planning is reflective activity, a problem-solving thought process—whereby past experiences and present facts are analyzed and projected to predict future trends.

4. Principle of Flexibility:

A good plan is that is sound but not rigid. It should be one that has sufficient scope for changing it from time to time.

5. Principle of Contribution to Enterprise Objectives:

Like all other plans, marketing plans must contribute positively towards the attainment of the enterprise objectives.

6. Principle of Efficiency:

Marketing Planning should facilitate the attainment of enterprise objectives at minimum cost and least effort while being able to absorb shocks and effects of unexpected developments.

7. Principle of Selection of Alternatives:

All Planning is decision making, choosing from among the available alternatives. While choosing the best alternative it should be that which contributes towards the accomplishment of goals most efficiently and effectively.

8. Principle of Planning Premises:

A plan is prepared on the basis of some foundations or against certain backdrops/in contextual reference to something known as 'Planning Premises'. Marketing managers and managers of other departments must agree on the premises of marketing plans.

9. Principle of Timing and Sequence of Operations:

Determination of start and finish timing for each task according to some definite schedule helps to shape actual performance in a concrete manner. .

10. Principle of Securing Participation:

Whole-hearted co-operation of employees in the execution of the marketing plan can be secured through timely communication and explanations of the plan to them. What is their role and where they stand in the bigger picture must be clearly conveyed to them.

11. Principle of Pervasiveness:

Though overall planning for a firm is the job of the top management, planning for department and unit levels is a function that must be performed by every manager in the organisation.

12. Principle of Strategic Planning:

Strategic planning must be carried out in the light of what the competitors are doing/ intending to do. This is necessary for accuracy in planning.

13. Principle of Innovation:

Innovation is necessary to ignite, retain and spark customer interest in products and services. It is the only way in which sustainable growth can be achieved.

14. Principle of Follow-up:

A proper follow-up system in the planning process will reveal the need to revise/adapt/drop/alter plans. Such timely changes planning make it more effective.

While these principle govern Marketing Planning, there is no one size fits all formula to plan. Planning would depend on:

1. The nature of work(quality, quantity, precision required, etc)

2. Time required for completion and how much time is available

3. Who will do it, How and in What sequence

4. What are the precedents in this regard

3.10 Steps in Marketing Planning Process

Marketing Planning is process which asks and seeks answers to the following questions:

1. Where are we now?

2. Where do we want to be?

3. How might we get there?

4. Which way is best?

5. How can we ensure arrival?

According to Philip Kotler the preparation of a good marketing plan involves the following stages:

1. Diagnosis: This involves asking "Where are we now?" and determining where the firm stands right now in terms of its resources, capabilities, and product/brand arsenal and market share. Data relating to company sales, market share, costing, plant capacity and utilization, profits will help a firm to answer questions as to why it is standing where it is in the present moment. A SWOT (Strength, Weaknesses, Opportunities and Threats) Analysis should be carried out.

Kotler suggests there are six specific dimensions of interest to the auditor:

External environment – macro and micro

Internal environment – covering:

- Marketing strategy
- Marketing organization
- Marketing systems
- Marketing productivity
- Marketing functions

2. Prognosis: This requires a firm to answer the question – "Where do we want to go?". This helps a firm to understand where it is headed, whether the future looks promising/bleak. The company also decides who its competitors are, what its product portfolio will be and

who its customers are through the STP process – segmentation, targeting and positioning.

The organization needs to examine its **portfolio** of products or companies and decide what strategy to adopt – for example, whether to grow or divest a particular product.

A product portfolio is comprised of all the products which an organization has. A product portfolio may comprise of different categories of products, different product lines and finally the individual product.

The STP model is useful for creating marketing communications plans because it helps marketers to prioritise propositions and then develop and deliver personalised and relevant messages to engage with different audiences.

Market **segmentation** is the process of dividing a market of potential customers into groups, or segments, based on different characteristics. The segments created are composed of consumers who will respond similarly to marketing strategies and who share traits such as similar interests, needs, or locations.

Targeting in marketing is important because it's a part of a holistic marketing strategy. It impacts advertising, as well as customer experience, branding, and business operations. Through targeting you can speak directly to a defined audience.

Through product positioning a company can make a brand occupy a distinct position, relative to competing brands, in the mind of the customer.

3. Objectives: If the prognosis does not reveal good prospects then a revision of marketing objectives is necessary.

4. Strategies: these are competitive/tactical plans that help a firm to meet the challenges posed by competition/ limited resources/sudden changes. For instance

premium pricing, new product development, diversification, digital advertising, brand associations with events/festivals are all examples of marketing strategies firms may adopt.

5. Tactics: these are methods to carry out strategies. For instance digital advertising versus traditional advertising could be a strategy used by a firm with limited advertising budget. Such a firm might opt to advertise on social media platforms and engage with audiences at a fraction of the cost of television campaign. These are tactics.

6. Control: Control is an essential part of the planning process. It ensures that everything proceeds according to plans and checks are in place to adapt to any sudden changes or shortfall in performance.

Broadly the steps in the Marketing Planning Process may be outlined as follows:

1. The first step in marketing planning process is the establishment of marketing objectives and devising marketing plans, policies, strategies and tactics.

2. The second step is designing the marketing system wherein the company designs/defines each function and its expected contribution towards the achievement of objectives.

3. In the third step, separate objectives, programmes, and strategies of each function are defined. This facilitates the assessment of their contribution towards the attainment of broader objectives. This helps to indentify the need for any modifications/adaptations that may be required in any particular functional area.

4. The fourth step entails drawing up detailed plans for each function for a shorter periods of time- weekly, monthly, quarterly,

halfyearly, annual. This helps in the definition of responsibilities, time and costs necessary to achieve short-term objectives.

5. The fifth and final step is merging marketing plans with organisational plans.

3.11 Relevance in Marketing Planning

Marketing planning should be relevant to:

1. **The Internal and External Environment**: This includes the firm's resource capabilities and the context in which it is operating, future trends and projections. Such an overview and analysis helps a firm to psot opportunities nad take advantage of the same.
2. **Competition:** Marketing Planning would be totally unnecessary had it not been for competition. A relevant marketing plan always takes the competition into consideration.
3. **Organisational Goals:** Planning should be in alignment with the organisation's goals/objectives and resources.
4. **Future projections and trends:** Planning is always for the future and should be in sync with forecasts and projections.
5. **Customer Expectations:** These expectations must be assessed and predicted in the context of the future. In order to attract customer interest in future, products should be made for the times to come.

3.12 Structure of Marketing Plan

The Marketing plan is the Blue print for marketing action. It revolves around the achievement of marketing goals and objectives; it outlines programmes and strategies to achieve the same. The 4 pillars of a marketing plan are Product, Price, Physical Distribution and Promotion.

The Marketing plan includes the following:

1. **Executive Summary:** gives readers an overview of the plan by summarizing each of the other sections of the marketing plan.

2. **Situational Analysis (Industry/Domain Specific):** This defines where the firm stands in relation to its competitors. You could be a new entrant or an established brand/company/unit. Since marketing planning aims at bridging the gap between where you are and where you want to be in future an analysis of internal and external environment, resources and capabilities provides the contextual background for objectives, plans, policies, procedures, programmes, strategies and tactics.

3. **Customer Profile:** Defines the target market. It outlines customers in various groups based on how they think, shop, behave, aspire with regard to the products/services you are offering. This section presents a demographic and psychographic profile of the target market.

4. **USP (Unique Selling Proposition):** A strong unique selling proposition (USP) is what distinguishes your product/service from competitors. For example: A Diamond is Forever (DeBeers) When it absolutely, positively has to be there overnight (FedEx Corporation) Drinks and Memories (Paper Boat) Book Unique Places to Stay and Things to Do (AirBnB).

5. **Pricing and Positioning Strategy:** Positioning refers to the place in the mind of the target audience- what sort of brand recall are you seeking. Nike for instance instantly reminds people of sporting goods but it hardly ever asks people to buy Nike products. Price can be a determinant for

a brand. The house of parle is known for the very affordable Parle G biscuits. In 2017 it introduced Parle Platina, a premium and exclusive range from the House of Parle. It included Hide & Seek, Milano, Mexitos, Friberg and Nutricrunch.

6. **Distribution Plan** A firm's distribution plan outlines how customers can buy the product/service. Options include directly via website? Or from distributors or retailers

7. **Financial Projections:** This should include an income statement, a cash-flow projection, and a balance sheet. The income statement includes the company's monthly financial performance and covers operating and non-operating costs.

3.13 Constraints to Effective Marketing Planning:

There are number of constraints to Marketing Planning. Some are internal while others are external.

1. **Too many Alternatives**: Marketing Planning is a choice making activity. One must choose the most efficient and economical course of action from among the available alternatives. Since there could be many way of achieving an objective this can create a problem of excesses-too much choice, thereby making it difficult to choose.

2. **Frequent Changes in Costs:** Costs depend on a number of external factors. Frequent changes in costs impact the efficacy of planning.

3. **Difficulties in Marketing Research**: Adequate information is the basis of good planning. Though the function of Marketing Research provides information for planning there are a number of difficulties in research. It is impossible to predict consumer behavior with accuracy. Further demographic, technological, economic, political and socio-cultural factors are transient and

difficult to control. Proper analysis of information is necessary for accuracy in forecasting which is the basis for planning.

4. **Changes in Government Policy:** This can prove beneficial or detrimental to an organisation. Changes in taxation/industrial/investment policies can promote/inhibit growth. For instance the recent Indo-China tensions have resulted in a ban on Chinese apps creating immense possibilities for burgeoning growth of Indian apps.

5. **Expenditure:** Marketing Planning is costly in terms time, energy and money.

6. **Incompetent Managers:** Only competent managers can plan and implement plans properly. The intelligence and abilities of marketing managers impacts the quality of plans. If managers are incompetent poor performance will reflect in faulty plans.

7. **Failure to Prioritize Objectives:** Planning is goal/objective oriented. If objectives are not prioritized properly plans will stand on a shaky foundation. The Maggi noodles comeback is a good example of proper prioritization of objectives.

8. **Hostile Corporate Cultures and Organisational Barriers:** The organisation should have an open, forward looking approach and friendly environment. In the absence of a good working environment people will find it difficult to work, stay motivated and implement plans effectively.

9. **Isolating the Marketing function from Operations:** Integration of the Marketing Plan with that of the Organisation is necessary. If managers insist on isolating the marketing function from all other functions, balancing resources and people becomes a big problem.

CASE STUDY: MAGGI NOODLES

Maggi Noodles launched in India in 1983. Over time the brand built a cult like following among mothers, children, youth and anyone who wanted a quick, hot meal. From the number one brand to zero sales trouble began for Maggi in 2015. Her's how effeicient marketing planning helped them in 2 ways:

1. To engineer a successful comeback
2. To undertake product diversification

In 2015 Maggi trouble began with The Food Safety and Standards Authority of India (FSSAI) imposing a nationwide ban on Maggi due to the presence of a high amount of lead and Monosodium Glutamate (MSG) in the noodles. Before the ban, the company enjoyed around 80%-90% market share but after the ban, its share plunged to zero.

The countrywide ban on Maggi was lifted was lifted by the Bombay High Court on 13 August 2015 and in the next year i.e. 2016, Maggi was relaunched in the Indian market by the Nestle India after getting the clearance certificate from the National Accreditation Board for Testing and Calibration Laboratories (NABL).

Regaining consumer trust is an uphill task. From being endorsed by Indian mothers now the problem was how to address Indian mothers concerns about what goes in to Maggi, Secondly, its celebrity brand endorsers did not want to be associated with the brand. Amitabh Bacchan, Preity Zinta and Madhuri Dixit were separately dragged to court for endorsing the brand.

Throughout the period of ban, Maggi did not stop communicating with consumers. They released a series of short films hashtagged #WeMissYouToo when it waited for the test results. Dedicated to all the fans who supported and stood by the brand, there was a Maggi fanboy/fangirl in each of the videos, who badly missed their favourite noodle. They are seen making a plea to Maggi, as if it were their long lost friend – "Come back, man!", "*Ab abhi jao*", "*kab wapas aayega yaar?*", "We miss you Maggi".

When the ban was lifted Maggi was made available for sale online exclusively on Snapdeal. Hashtags WelcomebackMaggi and

#SnapdealWelcomesMAGGI were trending.

In 2018, 35 years after Maggi noodles were launched in India, they have decided to go beyond a mother endorsing Maggi as good and convenient to make for her kids. After the Maggi noodles fiasco they also realized the importance of building a good arsenal of robust brands-going beyond their dependence on Maggi Noodles. The company planned to add new products to its dairy portfolio as part of its plan to reduce dependence on Maggi noodles that accounted for about 30% sales in 2014. As part of the product diversification effort, Nestle launched a range of greek yoghurts under the brand name of NESTLÉ a+ GREKYO.

NESTLÉ a+ GREKYO is available in several variants such as strawberry, mango, pineapple and orange. Apart from new variants of instant noodles, Nestle India will launch variations of pasta, Nestea, baby food, coffee, masala tea mix, chocolates and confectionery and many more products in a bid to reduce its dependence on Maggi.

Following the ban, Maggi clawed back to the top spot with around 55.5% of the market share, it is still far away from its hey days when it commanded 77% of the Indian noodles market and contributed around a third to Nestle India's revenues

This they achieved with their campaign of tastemaker Masala-ae-magic made by advertising agency Publicis India. The bigger picture which the campaign projects is one of social change, where women in India and their voices are becoming prominent. This Masala-ae-Magic campaign was promoted on television and digital. Alongside this the instant noodle brand Maggi opened the doors of its factories and kitchens for consumers. Nestle's web series titled "From Our Kitchen To Your Kitchen", featured the foodie duo Rocky and Mayur is an effort to help consumers to learn about Nestle's products and how they are made. The first episode featured Rocky and Mayur spending time to understand how Maggi is made in the company's manufacturing unit. The objective was showcasing the journey of the product starting with sourcing raw materials to manufacturing. To address concerns and questions about the role it plays in your diet. This campaign leveraged 24x7 consumer engagement services team and the company's digital—www.maggi.in.

In January 2019 after the Supreme Court revived the class-action suit by the government against the company in the National Consumer Disputes Redressal Commission (NCDRC), the company released a series of ads with the theme "Trustworthy facts" The print ads were an effort to highlight the company's approach as a credible, trustworthy and responsible company which communicates facts to consumers with simplicity and transparency.

CHAPTER 4:
MARKETING RESEARCH

4.1 Introduction

4.2 Meaning of Marketing Research

4.3 Definition of Marketing Research

4.4 Scope of Marketing Research

4.5 Role of Marketing Research

4.6 Marketing Research Agencies

4.1 Introduction

We know that marketing revolves around the consumer. Information is the fuel that drives marketing activities in the right direction. Marketing research presents the complete analysis of the market. Information regarding various aspects of the market such as size, nature, profitability, dynamics and a study of various factors- socio-economic, demographic, legal, political-affecting those aspects and any changes thereof. The objective of marketing research is to collect comprehensive information about consumers, competitors and the environment and markets for a firm's products or services. The ultimate goal is the provision of better products and services, an improved marketing mix and effective plans and policies to enhance the efficacy of marketing activities.

Marketing research is an activity/set of activities, a process, a method/method/s/technique/s/a combination of all these. Market Research and Marketing Research are terms people use synonymously but there is a difference in meaning and scope. Market Research is a sub-function of Marketing Research. Marketing research is a quest, a process of discovery wherein questions relating to the what, why, where, when and how of marketing are answered.

4.2   Meaning of Marketing Research

Marketing research may be described as a method of getting facts to be used by the executive in formulating policies and plans. It can also be defined as the systematic gathering, recording and analysis of data about problems relating to marketing of goods and services.

It is a systematic search for information. It involves data collection, analysis and interpretation. Research cannot draw decisions, but it helps the marketers in the task of decision making. Marketing Research eliminates the element of guess work and bias to facilitate objective decision making.

Marketing Research answers the following questions:

1. Who are your customers?

2. Where do they live?

3. How do they buy?

4. When do they buy?

5. Are they satisfied with your product/ service?

6. Who are your competitors?

7. How do you fare in comparision with your competition?

8. What are your competitior's policies and strategies?

4.3   Definition of Marketing Research

"**Marketing Research** is the systematic gathering, recording and analyzing of data about problems relating to the **marketing** of goods and services." **American Marketing Association** (**AMA**)

"**Marketing research** is a systematic problem analysis, model building and fact finding for the purpose of improved decision-making and control in the **marketing** of goods and services." **Philip Kotler**

"The careful and objective study of product design, markets and such transfer activities as physical distribution, warehousing advertising and sales management. Thus the scope of marketing research lies in its variety of applications." Marketing Research defined by **Clark and Clark**

Marketing research is also defined as, "The systematic, objective and exhaustive search for the study of the facts relevant to any problem in the field of marketing."

> *Features of Marketing Research:*
> 1. *Systematic Process*
> 2. *Analytical process*
> 3. *Problem Solving Approach*
> 4. *Enhances the efficacy of marketing activities*
> 5. *Sharpens Marketing Plans and Vision*
> 6. *Facilitates Decision Making*
> 7. *Holistic study of all elements of the Marketing Mix*

4.4 Scope of Marketing Research

1. Market Research: This involves data collection and analysis of market trends, market share and market potential. It is a comprehensive study of the market in terms of its size, location, nature and characteristics of markets. Markets are segmented on the basis of demographic variables like age, gender, income, education, occupation, socio-cultural factors like religion and psychographics like attitudes, values, interests, opinions, etc. Market research deciphers the "who, what, where, when, why and how" of existing and potential buyers.

2. Sales Research:
The sales and profitability are inter-dependent and are the very

basis for the existence of any commercial entity. Marketing is successful only when a firm is able to sell and enhance profitability. Sales research encompasses-sales forecasts, sales quota, sales territory design and other sales related activities. Further it analyses sales volume, performance of sales staff/sales territories, new product performance in test markets, customer related data etc.

3. Product Research:

The product/service is the core of the offering that a firm makes to the market. Product research comprises product planning and development, diversification, product line extensions, trimming product lines, revamping brand image, product testing, test marketing of new products etc. It involves the analysis of the strength and weakness of existing products in relation to diversification, simplification etc.

4. Advertising and Promotion Research:

This includes research of media, copy research, merchandising, packaging and measuring the effectiveness of various methods of advertising and promotion being employed against those which could be alternatively considered.

5. Corporate Growth Research:

This is the study of the entire firm/organisation in terms of it economic and technological forecasting, company image, location, profitability, merger, acquisitions, etc.

6. Business Economic Research:

This includes economic forecasting and business trend analysis, Marketing Planning, Marketing Mix and Profitability Analysis.

4.5 Role of Marketing Research

The role of Marketing Research can be understood from the point of view of who it benefits and how. Marketing Research benefits: manufacturers, distributors, advertisers and the government. Its role can be explained as follows:

1. Manufacturers and Marketing Research:

Marketing Research facilitates better decision making for manufacturers with regard to product planning and development, procuring material, plant location, planning, utilization of capacity and resources, controlling wastage, etc.

It provides inputs necessary for manufacturers to devise appropriate marketing strategies with respect to product, price, promotion and physical distribution.

2. Distributors and Marketing Research:

Marketing Research equips distributors with necessary information to be able to market the product/service better. It helps them to enhance personal selling, store layout, display, reach, store location, image and related factors to enhance brand loyalty and preference.

3. Advertisers and Marketing Research:

4. With the help of information provided by Marketing Research Advertisers can take better decisions relating to budgets, content, message, media, reach, frequency, media scheduling and media mix. The idea is to be able to optimize results through the use of the right media and message.

5. Government and Marketing Research:

Government has the important task of marketing ideas to promote social harmony, responsible citizenship and encouraging people to pay taxes among other significant tasks. In countries where modes of transportation are owned by the state or public-private partnerships the government will have to advertise the same. The government is also required to promote state/national tourism and marketing research helps in this.

4.6 Marketing Research Agencies

AMarketing Research Agency is a company offering market research services to clients. It is manned by a group of researchers and possesses an administrative infrastructure.

Top Marketing Research Companies in the world:

Nielsen, Kantar, QuintilesIMS, Ipsos, Gfk, IRI, Westat, Wood Mac Kenzie, Intage and Dunnhumby

Marketing Research Agencies may offer qualitative research, quantitative research, or both. These services could be supplemented by services like consultancy, facilitation of workshops and the like. Agencies may be micro/small scale/qualitative specialist agencies employing one or two individuals to large scale ones employing several hundred people.

Broadly there are 3 types of Market Research Agencies:

1. Field Service Market Research Agencies/Fieldwork Firms

They work with the target audience posing specific questions via interviews, focus groups, observation, surveys, and so on. They actually engage with respondents and collect data. Such agencies are often hired by other market researchers that already have a designed study to actually get answers from the target audiences. The data collected is then passed on to the researcher to analyze and draw insights from.

2. Intercept and Mystery Shopper Market Research Agencies

Such agencies are specialized field service firms that collect data in consumer markets at the ground level. The difference between them and Fieldwork Firms is that these firms specialize in face-to-face interaction with respondents for intercepts or carry out research through mystery shopping.

Companies who are looking for in-the-moment reaction from

buyers or those desirous of measuring actual customer experience across locations usually opt for such research agencies. These agencies utilize online intercept tools with mobile and beacon technologies to carry out their work.

3. Full Service Market Research Agencies

These agencies provide end-to-end customized market research services. Right from identifying the marketing problem, determining optimal research design, preparing instruments and methods, sampling, data collection, analyzing and reporting, they provide everything needed to carry out robust and comprehensive research. They assist businesses with the implementation of insights gathered and meet the demand for actionable research outcomes.

In addition to the 3 types of market research agencies highlighted above, there are also firms that sell research reports.

4.7 Marketing Information Vs. Marketing Research

Marketing Information provides the basis on which marketing decisions are taken. The quality and efficacy of decisions taken by a firm can be enhanced through the provision of qualitative information. The Marketing Information System refers to the systematic collection, analysis, interpretation, storage and dissemination of the market information, from both the internal and external sources, to marketers on a regular, continuous basis.

MIS is the establishment and maintenance of a permanent system (network) to provide decision makers across the organisation with the information they require on a regular basis. The system comprises people, facilities (gadgets/tools/equipment), and procedures that work in unison to collect, analyze, evaluate, distribute, collate and maintain updated information with the objective of aiding marketing decision-making, i.e., analysis, planning, implementation, and control of marketing activities.

MIS comprises parts, subparts or subsystems, called the components. These components are interrelated and interdependent. According to Philip Kotler, the MIS typically consists of four interrelated components – Internal Reports (Records) System, Marketing Research System, Marketing Intelligence System, and Marketing Decision Support System.

Thus it is evident that Marketing Research is just one component of the MIS. It is a part of the whole, a subsystem. The scope of Marketing Research is restricted to the problem it is trying to solve/ something that needs immediate attention. A particular problem could be a one-time study whereas the MIS is a permanent system that works regularly to ensure that information is always available. Marketing Research is limited to the study of specific problems, opportunities or situations. It's context is definite. Simply put, MIS is like an ocean and Marketing Research is a drop in that ocean.

4.8 Objectives of Marketing Research

Marketing Research works towards the fulfillment of the following objectives:

Product Oriented Objectives:

1. To evaluate the advantages and limitation of existing products/product lines/service offerings.

3. To study the level of acceptance/satisfaction/dissatisfaction of customers with regard to company products/services.

4. To estimate the market potential for new products.

2. To discover new forms/methods of packaging through comparison with similar packages.

Price Oriented Objectives:

1. To study price trends.

2. To facilitate competitive pricing.

3. To formulate offers/discounts.

Physical Distribution Oriented Objectives:

1. To evaluate the existing system of distribution.

2. To explore alternative systems of distribution and logistic support/means.

3. To study the nature of the market, its location and potential.

4. To explore and devise solutions to problems of marketing products/services.

Promotion Oriented Objectives:

1. To evaluate the reactions of consumers to existing products/services.

2. To measure the effectiveness of advertising.

Competition and Market Oriented Objectives:

1. To understand the impact of economic factors on sales volume and the opportunities created thereof.

2. To understand the competitive position of products/services of rival brands.

3. To estimate and analyze market share and potential.

4. To estimate future demand.

5. To evaluate the profitability of different markets/segments.

6. To assess the volume of future sales.

7. To evaluate policies and plans most suited to the fulfillment of marketing objectives.

8. To keep track of developments in the fields of science and technology.

9. To determine the extent of complexity of the marketing function.

10. To assess the strength and weakness of the competitors.

4.9 Marketing Research Procedure:

Marketing Research Procedure comprises the following major steps:

1. Problem Definition
2. Statement of Research Objectives
3. Research Design or Designing the Research Study
4. Sampling
5. Data Collection
6. Data Processing and Analysis
7. Formulating Conclusion, Preparing and Presenting the Report

4.10 Problem Definition

The process of Marketing Research process begins with problem definition. A clear-cut statement of the problem may not be possible at the very beginning of the research process as only symptoms of the underlying problems could be obvious at that stage. Some explanatory research/preliminary investigation helps to clearly define the problem Clear definition of the problem impacts the direction, quality and impact of subsequent research efforts. Clarity in problem definition facilitates the formulation of proper research objectives, determination of the techniques to be employed, and the nature and extent of information to be collected.

For instance when the Tata group decided to enter the branded jewellery business with Tanishq the problem for them was how to break/shake the trust customers had in their family jeweller for generations to come. Simply raising issues of impurity uncovered by research would not help which is why they brought in karat meters and invited people to test their old jewellery at Tanishq stores. This helped people to see results for themselves-"seeing is believing" was the old adage they proved holds true even today and can be used by marketers to their distinct advantage.

Once the problem is defined the researcher must clearly state research objectives in qualitative/quantitative terms and express the same in the form of a research question/statement/hypothesis.

4.11 Research Design

Research design is the framework for implementation of the research plan. It is a master plan that specifies research objectives, methods for data collection and analysis, time, costs, responsibility, probable outcomes, and actions.

Aspects/contents of research design may be broadly outlined as:

1. Statement of Research Objectives

2. Type of Data required

3. Definition of Population and Sampling Methods

4. Specifications of Time, Cost and Responsibilities

5. Methods of Data Collection

6. Data Analysis Methods/Tools

7. Probable Output/Outcomes

Types of Research Design

The type of Research Design to be used depends on the type of problem being studied. Broadly there are 3 types of Research Designs:

1. Exploratory Research Design:

Exploratory Research aims at the discovery of ideas/insights/aspects of the research problem. It is used by researchers in the initial stages of the study to familiarize them with the problem or to establish priorities among competitive explanations. It helps to clarify concepts for problem definition and developing hypotheses. It is fairly flexible.

2. Descriptive Research Design

Descriptive Research involves describing the problem and identifying solutions. It is more specific in terms of the who, what, where, when and how of the research problem. Unlike exploratory research it is not flexible, It rests on one or more hypotheses.

3. Experimental Research Design

Experimental Research aims at establishing the cause and effect relationship between certain variables/factors/phenomenon. It may involve manipulation of variables like price to determine its impact on demand for a product.

4.12 Data Collection

Data - factual information (such as measurements or statistics) that are used as a basis for reasoning, discussion, or calculation.

Data can be qualitative or quantitative.

- **Qualitative data** is descriptive information (it *describes* something)
- **Quantitative data** is numerical information (numbers)

Primary data: **Data** collected first hand by the researcher for a specific purpose. For instance: **Data** collected by a company from its dealers/stockists/customers. Primary data collection is carried out via surveys, interviews and experiments.

Secondary data: **Data** collected by someone else via surveys/experiments for some other purpose that is utilized by the researcher in his own study. Sources of secondary dats include: books, journals, magazines, newspaper articles/reports, research reports by other researchers/agencies/organisations, etc.

Sources of Data:

1. Internal: Data collection from company records, books of accounts, statements, etc.
2. External: Data collection from sources external to the company.

4.13 Sampling and Sampling Designs

Let us understand what is sampling. Sampling is the technique of selecting individual members or a subset of the population (total items) to draw conclusions from them and estimate characteristics of the whole population. Sampling is convenient and saves time and cost in research and is the foundation of a sizeable number of research studies.

Population could be described as a comprehensive group of individuals, institutions, objects and so on that have a common characteristics and are of interest to a researcher. A Census is a survey carried out to collect data from the entire **population.** However a census may be time consuming, impractical and over ambitious if the population is very large. Hence sampling becomes necessary.

Sampling design is a mathematical function that gives researchers the probability of any given sample being drawn. It is a critical part of statistics; It can be very simple or very complex. In the simplest, one there is no explicit stratification and a member of the population is chosen at random; each unit has the probability of becoming a part of the sample

A sample design comprises two elements.

- **Sampling method**: These are the rules and procedures by which some elements of the population are included in the sample. Some common sampling methods are Simple Random Sampling, Stratified Sampling and Cluster sampling (discussed in detail in the latter part of the chapter)

- **Estimator**. The estimation process for calculating sample statistics is called the estimator. Different sampling methods may use different estimators. For instance the formula for computing a mean score with a simple random sample is different from the formula for computing a mean score with a stratified sample. Similarly, the formula for the standard error may vary from one sampling method to the next.

There is no hard and fast rule as to which sample design must be used. The "best" sample design for your study might not be the best for another study. The sample design you use depends on research objectives and on resources at the disposal of the researcher. For instance a clinical study on a disease or drug trail will demand a higher level of precision and may require more commitment in terms of time, money and resources. On the other hand a department store that wants to study the efficacy of its layout/personal selling/window/store display can carry out a study with very low investment of time, money and through observation vis a vis a questionnaire and personal interviews which may be time consuming. If time and money are constraints a researcher may choose the design that provides the greatest precision without going over budget.

Sampling methods are broadly classified as probability and non-probability sampling:

1. **Probability sampling:** is a sampling technique in which a researcher sets a selection of a few criteria and chooses members of a population randomly. In probability sampling every member of the population has an equal opportunity to be a part of the sample.
2. **Non-probability sampling:** In this technique, a researcher chooses members for research at random. The selection process is not fixed or predefined. Due to this all elements of a population do not have equal opportunities to be included in a sample.

4.14 Probability Sampling Techniques

As explained earlier Probability Sampling is technique in which every member of the population has an equal chance/opportunity to be a part of the sample for the study. For instance if probability sampling is applied to a study of students enrolled in a college who may be 5000 in all, then every student of the college has a 1/5000 chance of being selected to be a part of the sample.

There are 4 types of Probability Sampling Techniques:

1. Simple Random Sampling: This is a reliable technique that saves time and resources in research. For instance if you want to study the shopping habits of students in a class of 500, you assign a number to each student and draw chits to select 50 students for the purpose of this study, this will be an example of simple random sampling.

2. Cluster Sampling: in this method researchers divide the population into clusters/sections. In the above example for instance if you decide to divide the population of 500 students into clusters based on gender/height/weight/city of origin, etc it would be an example of cluster sampling.

3. Systematic Sampling: let us consider the same example of 500 students from which you draw a sample of 50 and you say you will include every fifth student in your sample then this would be systematic sampling as you would be using a predefined range.

4. Stratified Random Sampling: in this type of sampling a researcher divides the population into smaller groups that don't overlap but represent the entire population. While sampling, these groups can be organized to draw a sample from each group separately. So out of 500 students you may want to study the shopping habits of students based on their occupational profile as to whether they are working/not working or their family income. So you can choose to study 25 students each of those who are working/not working or 10 students from each income group across 5 income groups defined by you.

Applicability/Use of Probability Sampling:

1. Reduces Bias in Sampling: it ensures higher quality data and proper representation of the population.
2. Ensures accuracy in Sampling
3. Diversity of population: Probability sampling is best used when the population is vast and diverse.

4.15   Data Analysis

Once data have been collected, they must be recorded, coded, classified and analysed appropriately. Invalid/incomplete responses must be eliminated before working on data analysis.

The preparation of tables, charts, graphs and diagrams helps to communicate findings better and must be employed in research. Suitable software for data analysis can be used. The interpretation of data analysis is equally if not more important. Interpretation must be carried out in the light of research objectives and the hypothesis/hypotheses (if any have been established). Assistance from statisticians may be sought if required and may prove to be helpful.

4.16   Method of Reporting Research Findings

The final stage in any research process is drawing conclusions, making recommendations and suggestions and presenting a report. A research report must be clear, specific, complete, fair and accurate. While preparing the report, the target audience must be considered. A brief write up on the contents of a report is included below:

(adapted from: John W. Best, Research in Education, 2nd ed., (Englewood Cliffs, NJ: Prentice-Hall, 1970)].

A. **Preliminary Section**
1. Title Page
2. Acknowledgments (if any)
3. Table of Contents
4. List of Tables (if any)
5. List of Figures (if any)

6. Abstract
B. **Main Body**
1. Introduction
a. Statement of the Problem
b. Significance of the Problem (and historical background)
c. Purpose
d. Statement of Hypothesis
e. Assumptions
f. Limitations
g. Definition of Terms
h. Ethical Considerations
i. Budget (proposal only)
j. Proposed Timeline (proposal only)
2. Review of Related Literature (and analysis of previous research)
3. Design of the Study
a. Description of Research Design and Procedures Used
b. Sources of Data
c. Sampling Procedures
d. Methods and Instruments of Data Gathering
e. Statistical Treatment
4. Analysis of Data
a. text with appropriate
b. tables and
c. figures
5. Summary and Conclusions
a. Restatement of the Problem
b. Description of Procedures
c. Major Findings (reject or fail to reject H_o)
d. Conclusions
e. Recommendations for Further Investigation
C. **Reference Section**
1. End Notes (if in that format of citation)
2. Bibliography or Literature Cited
3. Appendix

<u>CASE STUDY: ARIEL</u>

Procter & Gamble, a company with strong expertise in hand-washing spotted the opportunity in the detergent market in the 1960's, as the washing machine started to take off in certain countries. Women were happy with the ease of washing, but a new challenge appeared. Clothes weren't white enough. The P&G European Technology Center got to work. In 1967, Ariel arrived on the scene-with the USP- pristine whites thanks to an innovative combination of an enzyme based compound with encapsulated bleach.

They kept innovating as they went along- In 1985, the first liquid detergent from a P&G brand was released, the offering this time was- outstanding performance which could get rid of greasy stains.

In the 80's and 90's, consumers became more demanding and sought whites that were brighter than ever and an emphasis on no fading in case of colored clothes. This gave birth to Ariel Color, The 1992 innovation that offered women a bleach free, colour friendly option for their wash, brightening those colours instead of fading them.

Through all these innovations, Ariel has exhibited an understanding of how clothes can affect your life. Your favorite clothes are as important to you as they represent: happy memories, unforgettable stories and great moments lived together with your loved ones. Ariel as a brand is committed to helping customers preserve their clothes without worrying about stains and keeping the memories associated with those clothes alive.

In the 2000's the problem was not so much of having whiter and brighter clothes but one of paucity of time. The number of working women had increased and all women had one common problem-paucity of time. Hence Ariel's 2001 innovation, liquitabs were invented, gave women all over the world the quickest, easiest cleaning of clothes.

In 2012 they took this a step ahead with the innovative 3in1 Pods becoming the first and only 3 compartment liquid tab. Now Ariel had given women more time to spend on the important things – life, family and goals.

Ariel as a brand has worked on building a rock solid product that delivers unbeatable results. It has always focused on the problems faced by consumers and solved it with product performance be it whiter and brighter clothes and tough stain removal in one wash.

www.ingramcontent.com/pod-product-compliance
Lightning Source LLC
Chambersburg PA
CBHW071334140726
47996CB00005B/1963